GLOBAL SUSTAINABILITY

"The future of our planet depends on our ability to devise sustainable solutions through entrepreneurship. These practical examples of leadership show how companies can benefit from ethical business practices."

—**Sir Richard Branson**, Founder Virgin Group

"If you feel that your business requires you to choose daily between your conscience and your responsibility to your shareholders, you need to read *Global Sustainability—21 Leading CEOs Show How to Do Well by Doing Good*. It'll show you how to conduct business in a way that allows you to sleep at night … and just as important, how to justify your decisions to your investors."

—**Paul Polman**, CEO Unilever

"Mark Lefko was my CEO coach for nine years at Patagonia, and during that time I saw first-hand his passion for sustainability and leadership. With this book, he challenges other business leaders to discover how they can profit by sharing that passion."

—**Casey Sheahan**, Former CEO of Patagonia

"Sustainability is at the forefront in our minds. This book makes the seemingly complex theory of Global Sustainability easy to understand, and demonstrates that it isn't just some vague concept—it's a sound, necessary business strategy."

—**Ann Sherry**, CEO Carnival Australia

"After reading this book you'll understand how your company's well-being is inextricably linked to that of your customers, your suppliers, your employees, and the communities they live in. You'll also gain an appreciation of how these matters are interconnected, and how you can benefit from working at those intersections, "

—**Andrew Liveris**, Chairman & CEO
The Dow Chemical Company

"Mr. Lefko's inspiring and enlightening book must be required reading in every business school program! It neatly dispenses with the 'people vs. profit' dichotomy that has caused so much human misery for the last hundred years, and suggests a better, more profitable, more *sustainable* way of doing business."

—**Adlai Wertman**, David C. Bohnett Professor of Social Entrepreneurship and Founding Director of the USC Marshall Brittingham Social Enterprise Lab

"Through nine easy to understand and clearly articulated best practices Mark Lefko, in his new book on Global Sustainability, not only shows the way leaders can create sustainable businesses all over the world but how that in doing so they can positively increase their triple bottom line."

—**Robert ter Kuile**, Global Head of Sustainability Fossil Group

GLOBAL
SUSTAINABILITY

21 Leading CEOs Show
**HOW TO DO WELL
BY DOING GOOD**

MARK LEFKO

NEW YORK

NASHVILLE   MELBOURNE

GLOBAL SUSTAINABILITY
21 Leading CEOs Show HOW TO DO WELL BY DOING GOOD

Published in New York, New York, by Morgan James Publishing. Morgan James and The Entrepreneurial Publisher are trademarks of Morgan James, LLC.
www.MorganJamesPublishing.com

The Morgan James Speakers Group can bring authors to your live event. For more information or to book an event visit The Morgan James Speakers Group at www.TheMorganJamesSpeakersGroup.com.

Shelfie

A **free** eBook edition is available with the purchase of this print book.

CLEARLY PRINT YOUR NAME ABOVE IN UPPER CASE

Instructions to claim your free eBook edition:
1. Download the Shelfie app for Android or iOS
2. Write your name in **UPPER CASE** above
3. Use the Shelfie app to submit a photo
4. Download your eBook to any device

ISBN 978-1-68350-176-3 paperback
ISBN 978-1-68350-178-7 eBook
ISBN 978-1-68350-177-0 hardcover
Library of Congress Control Number:
2016912430

Cover Design by:
Rachel Lopez
www.r2cdesign.com

Interior Design by:
Bonnie Bushman
The Whole Caboodle Graphic Design

In an effort to support local communities, raise awareness and funds, Morgan James Publishing donates a percentage of all book sales for the life of each book to Habitat for Humanity Peninsula and Greater Williamsburg.

Get involved today! Visit
www.MorganJamesBuilds.com

DEDICATION

To my son Nathan, daughter Allegra, and all future generations who deserve the opportunity to have the resources and environment to thrive.

CONTENTS

ACKNOWLEDGEMENTS

Many people contributed to the creation of this book. Obviously, I owe particular gratitude to the CEOs and top executives of the leading companies that are featured in this book. They are committed and true leaders in the area of sustainability and were a big inspiration for me. They have given so generously of their time.

Andrew Liveris, Chairman and CEO The Dow Chemical Company
Ann Sherry, CEO Carnival Australia
Blake Mycoskie, Founder TOMS Shoes
Cyrus Mistry, Chairman Tata Group
Dave MacLennan, CEO Cargill
David Griswold, CEO Sustainable Harvest Coffee Importers
Feike Sijbesma, CEO DSM
Francois-Henri Pinault, Chairman and CEO Kering
Frank Dulcich, President and CEO Pacific Seafood Company

Guilherme Leal, Co-Chairman Natura

Jon Provisor, CIO Guidance Production

Marc Benioff, CEO Salesforce.com

Mike Kaplan, President and CEO Aspen Ski Company

Mike Sangiacomo, CEO Recology

Paul Polman, CEO Unilever

Phil Clothier, CEO Barrett Values Centre

Richard Branson, Founder Virgin Group

Ryan Devlin, Co-Founder This Bar Saves Lives

Seth Goldman, CEO Honest Tea

Tom Szaky, Founder and CEO TerraCycle

Walter Robb, Co-CEO Whole Foods Market

Please take a moment to look at the appendix in this book to see their photos.

The highlight of creating this book was my first interview with Paul Polman, CEO of Unilever in London. I am grateful for all of the time, inspiration, encouragement, and support I have received from him throughout this project. He was generous in making personal introductions and assisted me with access to many of the global multinational company leaders interviewed in this book.

I am grateful, as well, to the United Nations for their work in developing the Sustainable Development Goals (SDGs) which provided a great framework for this project.

My wife, Nikki Potter, and mentor, John Wood, who both have a huge passion for the topic of sustainability, were great sounding boards for this project and helped me to understand the depth of the issues we are facing around global sustainability.

My friends, Lawrence Koh, Ted Ning, Mark Samuel, Mike Hundert and Sherry Cefali connected me to CEOs in their network who were great interviewees for the book.

Two people spent more time with the manuscript than any other. Michael Levin and Bryan Gage were instrumental in structuring and organizing the vast amount of material gleaned from my interviews in order to present the stories and examples in a powerful and compelling way. Their support and counsel was invaluable and the book would not have happened without them. I am grateful for their hard work and dedication to this project.

Thank you to Mary Ellen Wojie, Barbara Lawton, Paula Patrice, George Foster, Wendy Armstrong, Helen Clarke, Hermine Kaesler, Gina Sheibley, Patty Vanderlin, Louis Vega, Mark Levy, Ben Walker, Beth Robson, Courtney Richardson, Gina Pogliano, Aukje Doombos, Priya Bery, Tiffany Gibson, Jenny Sommerfeld, Marissa DeCuir and Angelle Barbazon for their support in helping to bring my creative vision to life.

Finally, I want to acknowledge all the business leaders who understand that the time to address global sustainability is NOW and those who are doing something to participate in this growing movement.

INVITATION

"We are such spendthrifts with our lives. The trick of living is to slip on and off the planet with the least fuss you can muster. I'm not running for sainthood. I just happen to think that in life we need to be a little like the farmer, who puts back into the soil what he takes out."

—Paul Newman

What does the term *global sustainability* mean to you? If you're like most people, you probably haven't given it a lot of thought. It sounds like just another one of those buzzwords we hear in discussions about the environment—discussions many of us tune out.

But global sustainability is more than just an environmental concept; it's a business concern, and companies can profit by understanding and addressing it. Simply put, global sustainability means ensuring that all

Development. This agenda was adopted by all of the 193 countries making up the UN General Assembly on September 25, 2015.[1]

The program comprises seventeen Sustainable Development Goals that are targeted for completion by 2030. These include the reduction or elimination of poverty, hunger, and political inequality and injustice; stopping and reversing climate change; and providing everyone in the world with access to clean, potable water. Three of these goals have been assigned top priority: ending poverty, combating inequality and injustice, and combating climate change.

All these goals are linked to social issues—including climate change; this may seem counterintuitive, but problems with our environment have a direct impact on our ability to grow food and to create jobs, and this, in turn, raises poverty levels.

These clear goals and challenges were the inspiration for this book, and all of the twenty-one CEOs I interviewed were focused on addressing one or more of them. During these interviews we discussed what global sustainability means to them, what initiatives they have taken to advance it, and what they consider to be best practices for sustainability. I also asked them how their sustainability focus affects their company culture, and how they convince their shareholders, investors, and boards of directors to invest in sustainability. I wanted to get an idea how this book might encourage other leaders to take action and get involved.

Why Caring about Global Sustainability Is Good for Business

"Everything we do, we have a choice to either do it easy or do it right—and we've chosen to do it right every step of the way. As a result it's made for a much stronger brand for us, and much more

---

1 The United Nations website: http://www.un.org/sustainabledevelopment/sustainable-development-goals/

loyal customers. We've built a for-profit company that gives away a huge amount of money, but we're growing far faster and reaching sales goals far faster than we would've if we'd said, 'Let's not build giving into our model; let's just keep it all.'"
—**Ryan Devlin**, co-founder, This Bar Saves Lives

The UN isn't the only organization to have published a set of sustainability goals: Unilever, maker of such diverse products as Lipton® tea, Dove soap, and Hellmann's® mayonnaise, devotes a page of its website to its Sustainable Living Plan, which is designed "to make sustainable living commonplace."[2]

Unilever is just one of many, many companies that have come to understand the value of corporate concern about global sustainability, a meme so widespread that there is even a magazine devoted to it: *Corporate Knights*—the Magazine for Clean Capitalism. *Corporate Knights* was founded in 2002, and according to its website:

As one of the world's largest circulation (125K+) magazines focused on the intersection of business and society, *Corporate Knights* is the most prominent brand in the clean capitalism media space. We define "clean capitalism" as an economic system in which prices incorporate social, economic, and ecological benefits and costs, and actors know the full impacts of their actions.[3]

Recent decades have seen a sharp rise in public concern about the environment and about social issues. Littering became socially unacceptable during the 1970s, and since the early 1990s, Westerners have grown accustomed to separating their bottles, cans, and

---

2   Unilever website: https://www.unilever.com/sustainable-living/
3   *Corporate Knights*: http://www.corporateknights.com/us/about-us/

newspapers from the rest of their trash. More recently, sales of hybrid and electric cars have risen steadily ever since the day such vehicles first came to market.

The raising of public consciousness about doing what's right hasn't been limited to environmental issues: the term *fair trade* entered most coffee drinkers' lexicons in 2002, when the FAIRTRADE Mark began to appear on the packaging of any coffee brand that met the standards set by the Fairtrade International organization. Concern for the well-being of Third-World coffee farmers soon became the basis for the business models of importers like Sustainable Harvest° (a company whose activities we will discuss at greater length in a later chapter).

The PR benefits that accrue from being perceived by the public as a socially responsible company are incalculable . . . and indispensible, given the accountability engendered by the ubiquity of the Internet. If your company dumps a million gallons of pesticide into the Amazon River or uses Third-World slave labor to make cheap electronic devices, the public will find out; this kind of information can be gleaned at the tap of a button or the click of a mouse.

Successful businesses understand this, and so many of them go out of their way to demonstrate their social consciences to the public. It is for this reason that Cargill builds schools in Vietnam, while Virgin Group's Richard Branson devotes effort and money to preserving and sustaining lobster populations in the Caribbean.

Motive Doesn't Matter

Some might argue that these kinds of do-gooder initiatives are insufficient, or that they are motivated by cynicism because they are good PR, and the harm these companies may do outweighs or somehow negates the good they do. I disagree. It doesn't matter *why* a company is embracing global sustainability: it is important to acknowledge everyone who is focused on making a difference. I would submit that regardless of the reason you are embracing sustainability, it is a good thing. Judging the motives of a company is pointless anyway; how often does someone start out doing good for a self-serving reason and ultimately wind up being acknowledged for his efforts—which causes him to feel good, which causes him to more fully embrace the concept of selflessness, and the cycle continues until the desire to do good becomes part of his DNA. Such people are often the biggest true supporters of sustainability.

It is also easy to judge those CEOs who have not yet been fully successful at moving their companies to sustainable business practices. But I want to acknowledge those leaders who are at least trying in earnest to make something happen. It takes courage to expose oneself to criticism, and it is important for us to focus on progress and not perfection. The larger companies—especially giant multinationals—find it particularly difficult to make these kinds of changes: their challenge is akin to that of turning the direction of a supertanker. But all change needs to start somewhere. Business leaders are all human beings trying to find their way.

The companies in this book aren't perfect in everything they do, but they are displaying leadership in embracing sustainability. This, in turn, inspires their employees. They are finding that sustainability provides a good return on their investment, a return that would be worthwhile even if it were completely intangible. Ultimately, in business, it is about the triple bottom line: focus on people, profit, and planet—not just profit alone.

People, Profit, and Planet—the "Triple Bottom Line"

I would like to suggest that profit alone is at cross-purposes with global sustainability. It is an important driver in business, but in order to achieve global sustainability as defined, we also need to consider people and planet: people, because they are the most significant potential resources for innovation, invention, and creativity, and the planet, because we all need to have the environment to continue to be able to survive and work.

There is a term that speaks to this acknowledgement of these key components: the "triple bottom line." This term was coined in 1994 by a British businessman named John Elkington.[4] Elkington believed that businesses needed to attend to three distinct, separate bottom lines. The first of these is the traditional "bottom line" that everyone associates with this term: *profit.* The second bottom line is *people;* the organization should take some measure of its social responsibility. The third is *planet;* how big is the company's carbon footprint? According to the "triple bottom line" theory, only a company that minds all three P's can hope for long-term success in the twenty-first century business environment.

Conscious Leadership

In order to make the kinds of decisions that must be made for a company to fully embrace global sustainability, a business leader must practice what is called *conscious leadership.* Conscious leadership is leading with the awareness that whatever we say or do has an impact on everyone and everything around us. It considers all stakeholders—employees, customers, suppliers, investors, bankers, families, communities, society, and the planet—and has the intention of making decisions that are in the highest and best interest of all these stakeholders. Within the context of global sustainability, every person on the planet (and the planet itself) is a stakeholder, and should be considered when making decisions in business.

A conscious business leader focuses on the triple bottom line: people, profit, and planet. A conscious leader has a purpose that drives him or her and inspires the team. Conscious leaders are not perfect, but when they make mistakes, they clean them up right away. They have integrity

---

4   "Triple Bottom Line," *The Economist*, November 17, 2009 online extra: http:// www.economist.com/node/14301663

and strive to do the right thing for the benefit of all stakeholders. Conscious leadership is a key component necessary for the success of global sustainability. I would like to invite you to adopt a conscious leadership style and consider the importance of these qualities.

In the chapters that follow I will discuss in detail each of the best practices for global sustainability that I outlined at the beginning of this Invitation, and I will explain how each practice benefits not just the world at large, but also any business that adopts it. If you're still with me after reading all the lofty, altruistic business ideas I've been discussing for the last few pages, then I'll assume I have your full attention, and that you're open-minded, if not yet necessarily like-minded. Keep reading, and let's see whether we can bridge whatever gap may remain between us!

CHAPTER 1

ESTABLISH GUIDING PRINCIPLES

"People must have righteous principles in the first, and then they will not fail to perform virtuous actions."
—Martin Luther

The first and most important best practice for sustainability is to know what you stand for, and to be able to communicate your values to your employees, your customers, your shareholders, and the world at large. Who are you? What do you stand for? What drives you besides the bottom line? What commitments are you willing to make and stand by regardless of what happens? And are any of these commitments so vital to your company's identity that you are willing to keep them even at the expense of your ability to maximize profits?

1

These are not merely abstract questions; the answers will determine how you conduct your business for decades to come, both in lean times and during periods of prosperity. Your values must guide every business decision you make, and their importance to your brand cannot be overstated.

The Importance of Your Principles to Your Customers and to the Public

As I said, your guiding principles are inextricably linked to your brand, i.e., the public's perception of what you stand for. Your principles are the clearest signal you can send to indicate how you can be expected to act in the world. By establishing principles, you reassure every potential customer that he or she can support you with a clean conscience. Many of your customers—and perhaps even some of your suppliers—will decide whether to do business with you in large part based on their perception of you as a company that supports and upholds *their* values. And as I noted in the Invitation you've just read, the twenty-first century's easy access to information guarantees that if you fail to live up to your moral commitments, *your customers will find out!*

Perhaps the best, most explicit example of this practice in action can be seen with Cargill, the family-owned food-processing giant. I discussed this subject at length with CEO David MacLennan.

"It's the legacy of our founders and their descendants that they're committed to ethical business," he told me. "So there is complete support and buy-in. It's just part of the family-owned shareholder culture and ethos."

Cargill holds itself to seven "guiding principles," which it posts prominently on its website:[5]

---

5   http://www.cargill.com/company/ethics-compliance/index.jsp

1. We obey the law.
2. We conduct our business with integrity.
3. We keep accurate and honest records.
4. We honor our business obligations.
5. We treat people with dignity and respect.
6. We protect Cargill's information, assets, and interests.
7. We are committed to being a responsible global citizen.

Nor does Cargill stop with this strict code of corporate conduct: the company also features on its site the "Cargill Cocoa Promise," which offers reassurance to consumers concerned about whether their cocoa is obtained in an ethical manner. (We will discuss the Cargill Cocoa Promise at greater length in chapter 5.)

Cargill isn't alone in wearing its proverbial heart on its sleeve. The Indian multinational conglomerate Tata group displays its values prominently online, as do Unilever, *Natura Cosméticos* S.A., and The Dow Chemical Company. Tata's principles are expressed in a video, in which a voiceover tells us, "[O]ur mission [is] to improve the quality of life of the communities we serve globally through long-term stakeholder value creation based on leadership with trust—for customers, communities, employees, partners, and shareholders."[6]

> *"Our mission is at the core of our business, so we'd better make sure it's a live document. It's a live part of our business."*
> **—Seth Goldman**, CEO, Honest Tea

Salesforce, a San Francisco-based cloud-computing company, likewise prominently features its values on its website. The "About Us"

---

6 http://www.tata.com/Video/VideoPreview/Tata-groups-Vision-2025

link on the site's navigation bar brings up a list of options that includes an entire page about trust, and why they value it (there is also a link to a page dedicated to the subject of sustainability).

"This is our culture," Salesforce CEO Marc Benioff told me. "That is, we are a company that's committed to four things: One—trust, the trust with our customers, employees, and partners. Two—growth, because in the tech industry, if you're not growing, you're dying. Three—innovation; because we're a technology company, we're constantly innovating and delivering next-generation capability. And four—equality; we believe in equality for all, and we're willing to dedicate part of our time to our mission to help those who are less fortunate than we are."

Guilherme Leal, co-chairman of the board of directors at Natura, told me about Natura's Sustainability Vision (which also can be found on the company's website.[7])

"Natura wants to go further than just reducing and counteracting the impacts of its activities," he said. "We believe businesses must create net positive impact, which means contributing to regenerate nature and make society fairer than today. That's why in 2014 we developed a new Sustainability Vision. It directs our business to generate positive social, environmental, economic, and cultural impacts by 2050, and sets ambitions and commitments through 2020."

Leal isn't just blowing smoke here: Natura has been a member of the Union for Ethical BioTrade—which is dedicated to preserving biodiversity and ensuring fair dealing throughout supply chains—since the organization's founding in 2007.[8]

Unilever isn't at all coy about their commitment to sustainability; the section of their website devoted to the subject is conspicuously featured on the navigation bar at the top of every page.[9] By making their

---

7   https://www.naturabrasil.fr/en/our-values/sustainable-development
8   http://ethicalbiotrade.org/our-members/trading-members/
9   https://www.unilever.com/sustainable-living/

Sustainable Living Plan impossible for visitors to miss, the company sends an unmistakable message to consumers: global sustainability is a core value from which Unilever will never budge. And lest anyone mistake their promises for empty platitudes, Unilever spells out its own stake in solving the world's problems:

> [T]he changes [in climate, population, and resource availability] will pose new challenges for us too, as commodity costs fluctuate, markets become unstable and raw materials harder to source. There is no "business as usual" anymore. The old economic systems are no longer fit for purpose.

The Dow Chemical Company's website offers us a look at Dow's seven ambitious "2025 Sustainability Goals."[10] These goals, which Dow hopes to achieve within the next decade, include the development of "a circular economy where materials formerly considered to be 'waste' are turned into new products, and the goods we use every day are designed to be fully recycled."

In mentioning Dow's 2025 Sustainability Goals, Natura's Sustainability Vision, and Unilever's Sustainable Living Plan, I have perhaps strayed somewhat from the prescription I mean to offer in this chapter: to establish principles. But while the plans, visions, and goals touted by those companies are not *guiding principles* in the same strict sense as Cargill's, they still have the desired effect of clarifying these companies' resolve not to contribute to the world's problems. They also ensure accountability in the future: if Dow, for example, were to abandon its stated goals at some point a few years down the road, or if it were discovered not to have been taking them seriously, the public outcry would be enormous . . . and that would be bad for business.

---

10   http://www.dow.com/en-us/science-and-sustainability/sustainability-reporting

The Importance of Your Principles to Your Employees

> *"We found that by embracing sustainability, we were connecting more strongly with our employees. It really resonated with them. We were able to recruit and retain better talent. We were also doing a better job and gaining traction and . . . credibility within the community."*
> —**Mike Kaplan**, president and CEO, Aspen Skiing Company

It's admirable for a company to set ambitious goals, but it can only hope to *achieve* such goals if its employees are willing to adopt them as their own (this is one reason why employee well-being and morale will be the subject of an entire chapter later in this book). In order for this to happen, employees must have the sense that the company takes its principles seriously, and that these principles arise from sincerely held convictions. Most people are not utter fools, and no one likes to feel as though he or she is being lectured about the break-room recycling bin in order to stroke a supervisor's sense of moral superiority, or in order to burnish the company's image as a socially responsible corporate citizen.

On the other hand, employees who are inspired by the company's mission—and who understand the reasons behind that mission—will go to great lengths to further it. This can and should be taken into account from the time an employee is hired. Applicants should be favored who evince an affinity for the company's goals, not just in business (which of course is a job requirement), but also in matters of principle.

François-Henri Pinault, chairman and CEO of clothing and luxury-goods manufacturer Kering, told me, "[Our values dictate] every action, every decision that is taken in our business. [They] cannot be . . . taken into consideration [only] at some point of a process or at the end of a process, or in the middle. And as I said to my team . . . this is who we are. So, you cannot cheat with that. It's not an option. We are like this; we think like this; we breathe like this. And so everything has to be seen through this dimension of sustainability."

If you succeed in inculcating your employees with your company values, the results can be far-reaching. Cargill's David MacLennan told me this story when I interviewed him:

> I'll never forget, two years ago this July, I was at one of our facilities in Ukraine. And I walked in and there was a poster numbered one through seven, and there were pictures of employees on it. It was the same layout and color scheme [as the posters we hang in our United States offices], but everything was in Ukrainian. And we went upstairs, and on that person's desk was a copy of the guiding principles. And I thought, *That tells me something: that it's not me sitting in Minneapolis or our leadership team proclaiming our guiding principles; it's in the system.* And so I think the role of leadership is to say, "Here's what we think is important; here is above all else where we want to go and how we're going to conduct our business. And I have seen firsthand evidence that that resonates with people. It's cross-cultural.

Once they've become ingrained in your culture, your company's values and ethical standards will become a selling point with which you will be able to attract and retain talented, ambitious people. I asked Mr. Pinault whether his company's culture had any effect on the kinds of job applicants Kering attracted.

He said, "We transformed, years ago, our process of recruitment to involve questions about sustainability for all the candidates, to test their conviction about that . . . and [since we have become] more and more known as a sustainable company, and [since we have begun to ask] those questions, we have [received] amazing feedback from candidates who are very receptive. The young generation asks us questions about that before we [can ask them] our own questions about [their feelings about] sustainability. This is a very strong trend. They all come in with questions about that topic. So, it's very important, and in the future [it will be] one of the key components of [employee] loyalty that you can rely on as a company."

Mr. Pinault's experience is not unique: according to Unilever CEO Paul Polman, "Unilever gets 1.8 million applicants [per year]. We are the most looked-up company on LinkedIn after Apple and Google because these people want to work for a purpose, [and for] a company with a purpose. In fact, more than half of our recruits tell us that they join us because of our Unilever Sustainable Living Plan, and they want to make a difference."

Jon Provisor, CIO of Internet service provider Guidance, says, "I have had employees come and say, 'I joined Guidance because of your view on the environment.'"

Dr. Mukund Rajan is the chief ethics officer of the Tata group and oversees all corporate social-responsibility activities as chairman of the Tata Global Sustainability Council.

He told me about the response among Tata employees to a program designed to encourage volunteerism: "Some [of the employees surveyed afterward] felt that it was a very important part of being part of the Tata group, and they would volunteer again. Volunteering . . . is one of the easiest propositions for corporations to undertake. It doesn't cost a lot of money. People, particularly millennials, are increasingly interested in seeing that their employers really have a social conscience and [are] willing to volunteer. So value can be created through pro bono efforts."

"Our people feel there is a soul in the company; a purpose. And people want, I think, to work for a company that has a soul and a purpose. It has an effect not only internally, but also externally— for example, on talent recruitment, especially for the younger generation. They don't want to work for a company for the benefits or the pension package; they want to work for a company where they can say the values match with their own values."
—**Feike Sijbesma**, CEO, DSM

While principles are important, it is also important to remember that people are only people, and only human. Despite one's best intentions, and despite the most careful hiring practices, bad apples may be hired, or good employees—indeed, sometimes even the best employees—may experience lapses in their good judgment. David MacLennan told me this:

Sometimes your guiding principles are violated, and we're not naïve [enough] to think that with a large company with 150,000 employees [in] seventy countries, things always go the way that they should. What we [attempt to cultivate] is a culture of candor and a culture of openness, and we rely on the guiding principles for us to be in business and for us to be trusted. And [in] a values-based company, when you have a violation of your guiding principles, you need to move quickly to respond to it. [We had a situation] last week where [someone] didn't manage their budget . . . in a way which was consistent with our guiding principles, and they were asked to leave the company. And it was done quickly and without hesitation. I think how you respond [to violations of] your guiding principles is ultimately what defines your culture.

The Importance of Your Principles to Your Shareholders

Enacting and abiding by guiding principles can be challenging, not least because situations may sometimes arise in which it may appear to shareholders and others that you are losing money by sticking to your principles, at least in the short term. In this respect, small companies may sometimes have an advantage over big corporations. The collective will of countless shareholders can act as an impersonal force of nature, making it difficult or outright impossible for CEOs to follow the dictates of their consciences. A small operation, by contrast—or even a very large one, if it is privately held—is accountable to fewer people, and in some cases, CEOs may have no one's money at stake but their own. Coffee importer Sustainable Harvest®, for example, has no outside shareholders, which makes it easier for them to hold to the values on which their entire business model is predicated.

Blake Mycoskie is the founder of TOMS Shoes, and the brains behind the company's signature pitch—for every pair of shoes a customer buys, TOMS Shoes will provide a new pair of shoes to a disadvantaged child in Africa, Asia, South America, or some other part of the world where there is a need. He offered me this example of the advantage a smaller company has when it comes to standing on principle:

> For the first eight years of TOMS, I had no investors. And because I had no investors, I was not limited in the creation of all these programs and the creation of our business model, and I was able to build all that into the cost of the business. So when I went out to get investment partners, I said, "Look, here's the opportunity for us to grow. Here's how I think you can make a reasonable return on your investment. But also, just so you know, these are programs that we will always have, and this is part of our promise to our customers and our promise to our employees. And so if you're going to have any issue with

any of these cost centers, then TOMS is definitely not the right investment for you.

And so we found a partner that really could see that while, yes, these are cost centers, there's also a lot of marketing value for them, and there's a lot of value in our employees' engagement and satisfaction. And so they've been able to see that you really can run a business in the way we're doing, and that it can be profitable and can grow and can scale, but also stay true to its original commitment. Because that is what the brand is. So, it's really important for us to find an investor that just got it, that you wouldn't want [to change that business model] even if it looked good on the balance sheet or the profit-and-loss statement in the short term.

Cargill, on the other hand, is no small operation; in revenue terms, it is the largest privately held corporation in America. It is also 90 percent family owned, and has been in the control of its founders' families since its founding in 1865.[11] This, perhaps more than any other factor, is what allows David MacLennan the freedom and independence he needs to be able to insist upon adherence to the company's guiding principles. Even so, Mycoskie makes a good point when he says that you really can run a profitable, growing business at any scale without abandoning your principles. Even a giant, publically traded corporation can say of any or all of its principles, "This is vital to our business model and necessary to our long-term success. If you have a problem with these principles, or if you're just looking to make a quick buck, then this is not the investment for you." This reflects an aspect of another best practice: long-term thinking, which will be the subject of our next chapter.

---

11 *Forbes*, http://www.forbes.com/lists/2009/21/private-companies-09_Cargill_5ZUZ.html

Key Takeaways:

1. Your guiding principles are inextricably linked to your brand, i.e., the public's perception of what you stand for.
2. These principles must be featured prominently on your website.
3. Employees must buy into your principles.
4. A reputation for doing business in a principled, ethical way can help you attract and retain talented, valuable employees.
5. It is possible to do business in this manner on any scale.

$$\boxed{\longrightarrow \text{CHAPTER 2} \longleftarrow}$$

PRACTICE LONG-TERM THINKING

"If you're a leader [who] can really make a difference, then you should be asking yourself not only what kind of business legacy you're leaving, but what kind of human legacy you're leaving."
—**Mike Kaplan**, president and CEO, Aspen Skiing Company

Shortsightedness in pursuit of immediate profit not only damages society and the environment, but also harms the long-term profitability of a business. In some cases, an entire industry can be jeopardized by this kind of thinking. This is true both in terms of resource sustainability—imagine how long the timber industry would last if it never planted new trees to replace the trees it cuts down—and in financial matters. Businesses must plan for the future, and must not allow themselves to be sidetracked into the pursuit of short-term results and instant gratification.

Long-Term Thinking in Financial Matters

There is too much focus on short-term results in business today. Investors in the capital markets are driven by quarterly earnings, and this puts tremendous pressure on CEOs to develop short-term strategies to return quarterly profits at the expense of sustainable solutions that are in the long-term interest of all stakeholders. Because of this pressure, many CEOs fear for their jobs if short-term results do not meet expectations and stock prices are not growing. This pressure for quarterly results is in direct conflict with the necessity of long-term investment in initiatives that will support global sustainability.

"The investors of the '80s and '90s, and even until about ten years ago, they understood patient money," says The Dow Chemical Company CEO Andrew N. Liveris. "They understood R&D; they understood that you will not get income from today's R&D dollar. You're generating income from . . . today's investment [to achieve a] better standard ten years from now. That is not true anymore, and that is the biggest headwind that humanity collectively faces: that . . . the deployment of financial capital and the returns expected now are short-term, ninety-day returns—the death march every quarter. So the way the incentive structures are built right now, if you don't do short-term performance, there is no incentive structure that delivers financial rewards for long-term performance. So you've got to recalibrate that somehow."

The answer is, of course, some degree of balance between short-term earnings and long-term investments. Finding this balance will require courage on the part of CEOs and business leaders, who must communicate with shareholders, bankers, and other investors about the importance of ensuring that their investments are sustainable in the long run.

There seems to be a more patient and understanding investor base in Europe than in the United States. European companies like Unilever and DSM have been having difficult conversations with their investor base over the last ten years about investing in sustainability. Certainly, some investors have abandoned ship as a result, but these companies now tend to attract a new breed of investors who understand the importance of sustainability and are willing to accept a longer-term outlook. These investors understand that current investment is required in order to build momentum for long-term prosperity, and that this will have an impact on short-term returns.

Unilever CEO Paul Polman spoke to me at some length about this topic:

> The day I became CEO I abolished quarterly profit reporting . . . If we do the right things, [then] we do them for the longer term. We have to get out of this quarterly rat race, this expectation management versus reality. And that's a business model that's not run by quarters; that's a business model that's run by years.
>
> Now, since we don't report profits every quarter, the goals that we set are not just simple financial goals. Nor do I talk about that. Some people might say "Hey, you had a bad year because you only grew by 3 percent and your profit is only up 5 percent, while [your] competition has grown perhaps by 4 percent and their profits are up by 10 percent." I say, I don't know if that is a bad year. If your definition is a narrow finance definition, then yeah, you might interpret it as a bad year. If you are very short-term orientated and only look at twelve months, you might even be right.
>
> But if you believe in a long-term sustainable model, then why don't we look at it over five years or ten years? You might have connected with five hundred million more consumers, improving their lives and livelihood and [encouraging them to] become your loyal consumers in the next year or the year after. They will be your future consumers, and they won't forget you.

So [we] take a long-term perspective . . . if we invest in training, if we invest in information technology, or if we invest in factories that only pay out five or ten years later, why shouldn't we invest in the future of humanity? And if you do that in a way that is relevant to your business, perhaps that year was a very good year.

Along with Tata chairman Cyrus P. Mistry, Polman sits on the advisory board of an organization called Focusing Capital on the Long Term (FCLT), which has gathered a group of companies to address the need to focus less on short-term earnings pressure and more on long-term performance and growth in value. One of FCLT's objectives is to demonstrate that sustainable business practices don't have to be just a cost; rather, they can be more profitable in the long term. On its website, FCLT describes the problem with short-term thinking:

Business leaders argue that when companies forgo profitable investments to meet quarterly earnings expectations, investors and savers lose potential future returns. And all of us miss out on the benefits of long-term economic growth. The pressure to manage short rather than long is only increasing, leaders report. We believe that business leaders must and can act to reverse the short-term myopia that pervades modern business and market behaviour. [Our mission is] to develop practical structures, metrics, and approaches for longer-term behaviours in the investment and business worlds.[12]

When we discussed his involvement with FCLT, Mr. Mistry told me, "I firmly believe that living in a quarter-to-quarter world is

12 Focusing Capital on the Long Term website: http://www.fclt.org/en/theinitiative.html

inappropriate for a company. Hence we've developed an initiative by like-minded corporates and investors to look at how we build value for the long term. How do you look at different incentive structures . . . and how do you communicate with all the stakeholders?"

The Dow Chemical Company's Andrew Liveris, also a member of FCLT, says, "This mind-set [long-term thinking] has enabled Dow to increase returns on one-and two-year time horizons while making strategic investments that will deliver even greater profits ten or twenty years from now."[13]

Dutch multinational DSM likewise takes a long-term view of financial matters, as CEO Feike Sijbesma discussed with me during our interview. Sijbesma is a man of extraordinary intellectual and moral standing; he is a trained biologist and received 2010 Humanitarian of the Year Award from the United Nations Association of New York for his work with the United Nations' World Food Programme.

He told me, "We have a very clear dividends policy, and I put that strongly to shareholders. I promise to pay them a stable or slightly increased dividend every year, and that has to do with my trust that we move our business in the right direction and maintain stability. And, of course, our profit will fluctuate some years, but I would like to have a long-term journey. You do not join us for a rise in this quarter or the other quarter. If that is your investment policy, then maybe you should find other targets to invest in than us, please."

I heard this sentiment echoed by many of the CEOs I interviewed in the course of writing this book.

Blake Mycoskie, founder of TOMS Shoes, says, "It's really important for us to find an investor who just *gets* it. Even if it looked good on the profit-and-loss statement in the short term, you would never want to do something to mess with the integrity of how we do our giving,

---

13 FCLT website: http://www.fclt.org/content/dam/fclt/en/resources/
    InclusiveCapitalism.pdf

because if that goes, the brand goes. And what all these investors want—what they're investing in—is the brand value. So, they're going to make more money by TOMS Shoes growing its business and going into new categories, not by cutting our costs."

TOMS Shoes operates on a business model dedicated to philanthropy—the company's "One for One" giving program described in chapter 1—and it's important to Mycoskie for the company always to retain the flexibility to preserve that core element of its brand. This is a large part of the reason the company has never gone public.

"Private equity [is very different from] venture capital," Mycoskie says. "I think it would be very hard to work with venture capital, because venture capital's looking at very rapid increase in value, and very rapid growth, whereas private equity is more patient in nature and a little bit longer-term, and they're investing in stable businesses [for which] the risk is a lot lower, so they could have an actual brand that they've invested in, not just an idea. I think . . . we will be very careful if we ever do decide to go public [to be] very clear on our bylaws so shareholders understand that we're not going to run this business on a quarterly basis. And I think if you're really vocal about that in the beginning, then you attract only investors who understand that mentality and who will support [it]."

> *"We have always targeted long-term investors who are really engaged with our values, and I'm glad to say that we have succeeded. [During] my short participation in the IPO roadshow in 2004, I personally told potential partners that if they did not believe in the values we carry, they should not invest in our company, because this is our way to do business. Today . . . a new type of investor . . . is consistently showing that companies with triple-bottom-line management can offer greater returns."*
>
> —**Guilherme Leal**, co-chairman, Natura

Long-Term Thinking Also Means to Husband Resources for the Future

The obvious place to begin a discussion about this topic is to return to my earlier example about the timber industry, which plants roughly 90 percent of all new trees in America.[14] They do this not just because the law requires it—although it does—but also out of self interest: if new trees were never planted, eventually there would be no more trees, and no industry to profit from cutting them down.

This holds true for any industry that takes its product from the natural world. This is why Pacific Seafood, one of the largest seafood companies in North America, cares about the sustainability of marine resources.

"By understanding the biology and maximizing the recovery of each fish, we can harvest less fish and feed more people," says Pacific Seafood Group President and CEO Frank Dulcich. "We've learned how we have to harvest oysters in order to minimize the shock to them, and we're getting a 15 percent better recovery from our oysters due to our harvest methods." Dulcich also says Pacific Seafood has improved recovery on shrimp. "Since 1990 we have doubled our recovery," he says. "By studying the biology we have been able to double the sellable shrimp meat without catching more shrimp." This reduces the environmental impact of fishing (which, in turn, supports the long-term sustainability of fishermen's livelihoods, thereby establishing another bulwark against poverty in fishing communities), and obviously it's good for the company's financial bottom line.

Along similar lines, Richard Branson, founder of Virgin Group, is involved with an initiative called The V-Notch Sustainable Lobster Fishing Practice Program, which is dedicated to teaching Caribbean lobstermen a practice known as "V-notching," the purpose of which

---

14   Virginia's Sustainable Forestry Initiative Program: http://sharplogger.vt.edu/
virginiasfi/faq.html

is to preserve and sustain the population of egg-bearing/egg-producing lobsters. The idea is to mark egg-bearing females when they are caught by cutting a small, V-shaped notch in their tails, and then to throw them back into the water. When this practice is standardized in a community, other fishermen are expected to throw back any lobster they find with such a marking (whether it currently carries eggs or not). The marking generally lasts for about two years, and when it is used properly, the technique reduces overfishing and sustains lobster populations. Lobster populations off the coast of Maine that were threatened by overfishing have recovered since V-notching was implemented there. According to Branson, "Lobster landings in Maine have exploded from an annual average catch of twenty million pounds to ninety-five million pounds landed in 2010."[15] Branson's foundation is supplying the equipment and training to encourage Caribbean lobstermen to follow suit.

Just to be clear, Branson's activity here is activism motivated by goodwill, and it doesn't directly benefit him or Virgin, which is not in the seafood business. Teaching V-notching to lobstermen isn't an example of the practice of long-term thinking on Virgin's part; rather, the practice of V-notching itself is long-term thinking on the part of the lobster-fishing communities that implement it. The point is that there's a lesson to be drawn from the care these lobstermen take of the populations from which they draw their livelihoods . . . a lesson that is reinforced when you consider the example set by Pacific Seafood.

Additional examples abound throughout the corporate world of resource husbandry as an outgrowth of long-term thinking: Last year Natura launched a line of moisturizers and soaps made with the seed of the Ucuúba tree.

"The tree was used to make broomsticks and was threatened with extinction," says co-chairman Guilherme Leal. "Today, the sustainable production of its seeds generates three times more income for [Brazilian

---

15   https://www.virgin.com/richard-branson/v-notching

indigenous] communities than the fallen trunk. I'm glad to say that the sustainable use of Brazilian biodiversity is at the core of our business strategy. This has been one of our main areas of research and innovation since the early 2000s." This action on Natura's part is actually an illustration of *two* of our best practices for sustainability; the other practice concerns adaptability and a willingness to create and seize opportunities (we will return to this topic in chapter 8).

Other Examples of Long-Term Thinking

> *"We all can win if we just adopt more sustainable practices. Clean energy is a net win for everybody. Yes, it's a big initial investment, but it pays back in multiples over time. You could buy a junky car every three years for your whole life or you could buy a nice car that lasts you twenty years."*
> —**Ryan Devlin**, co-founder, This Bar Saves Lives

While I've used most of this chapter to make the case for long-term thinking about global sustainability as a matter of economic self-interest for businesses of all sizes, I think it may be appropriate at this point to remind the reader of what's ultimately at stake: the future of human life as we know it on this planet.

The high stakes we're playing for are certainly not lost on Richard Branson, who said to me, "We are thinking that 2050 should be the time that we're carbon neutral, and . . . we are now urging for a price in carbon.[16] You know, I've got a lot of airlines. It is not going to be in my short-term personal interest, but for the sake of the world, we need a price on carbon or else we're not going to get to carbon neutrality by 2050."

---

16 Carbon pricing: a proposed method for reducing global emissions that contribute to climate change.

Imagine what humanity could accomplish if all business leaders exhibited the kind of broad-minded, forward-thinking vision that has made Branson not only widely admired, but also richer than the average person can imagine in his wildest fever dreams.

And it's not just the environment that's at risk: political instability caused by poverty and injustice is a threat to global economic security, and therefore, a threat to the standard of living enjoyed by the entire developed world. In light of this, anything that can be done to lift people out of poverty and improve the long-term economic health of poor communities anywhere in the world contributes to global sustainability by creating markets in the future. Branson offers us an anecdote that illustrates how easy this can be to achieve:

"I was in South Africa having dinner, and this woman who was sitting next to me—she was a village elder—asked if there was any way I could lend her $200 to buy a sewing machine. I don't normally carry money, but I just happened to have $200 in my pocket, and I slipped it into her hand and assumed that was the last I was going to see of it. And she said, 'I'll be able to repay you in three or four months.'

"Anyway, about six months later, I was down there in the village and these four women came up to me and gave me this beautiful colored cape . . . and they gave me back the $200! And when I asked where the woman was, [they told me] she was in the marketplace selling produce. But all four of these women were now working full time for her. So, $200 had turned into five people's jobs."

I think it's safe to assume that the woman who was the beneficiary of Branson's spontaneous act of generosity is still running her business, and still growing it, lifting not just herself out of poverty, but her neighbors as well. And once people's lives have been enriched in this way, they quickly become consumers, i.e., potential customers.

The Dow Chemical Company's STEM Ambassadors program, launched in 2014, seems well designed to sow these kinds of seeds. The acronym STEM stands for Science, Technology, Engineering, and Math education, and according to the information they sent me, "Dow believes that a STEM-literate society will lead to innovation, growth, and economic prosperity" and that "investing in our youth is critical for the future of the chemical industry and our nation as a whole." The way the program works is simple: highly trained Dow employees volunteer their time in communities near Dow facilities, supporting teachers and inspiring students to pursue education—and eventually careers—in the STEM fields. The program began in the US and is now beginning to spread globally. According to Dow's website, "School day activities may include career talks, guest lecturing, science experiments, mentoring, and science research."

The Tata group has a similar program called Tata STRIVE, which is responsible every year for training tens of thousands of students in various trades—and Tata's website proclaims the company's intention to expand the program globally.[17] Charmingly, the page devoted to describing the STRIVE program opens with a quotation from the Buddha: "Thousands of candles can be lit from a single candle, and the life of the candle will not be shortened."

"If you don't solve something at the front end you'll pay double for it at the back end, either through fines, penalties, or audits."
— **Andrew Liveris**, CEO, The Dow Chemical Company

Most people think they understand what long-term thinking is, and why it's important, but we tend to practice it selectively. That kind of

---

17 Tata website: http://www.tata.com/sustainability/articlesinside/Striving-to-empower

myopia isn't going to cut it anymore. A business that focuses only on short-term profits will never grow to reach its true potential or achieve maximum profitability. And a people who don't consider the long-term consequences of their actions—and who fail to change direction when it becomes apparent that they're headed for a cliff—will not be long for this world. But if we recognize the return on investment we get from planning for the future and planting seeds in the gardens of the less fortunate, there is no limit to the profit we can realize.

> *"It's not just the right thing to do morally; you'll actually make more money down the road if you take a more sustainable approach. Your customers will be more like evangelists, your employees will be more engaged and productive, and you'll find that other businesses are more encouraged to partner with you because they like what you're doing. I always say, don't look at this as a cost; look at this as an investment with a very high ROI. It might be a longer-term ROI, but it will come."*
> —Blake Mycoskie, founder, TOMS Shoes

Key Takeaways

1. Shortsightedness in pursuit of immediate profit not only damages society and the environment, but also harms the long-term profitability of a business.
2. Short-term strategies to return quarterly profits often hinder sustainable solutions that are in the long-term interest of all stakeholders.
3. Short-term profit may sometimes need to be sacrificed in order to preserve long-term brand integrity.
4. Natural resources need to be sustainable in order for industries that depend on those resources to remain sustainable.

5. Sustainable business practices don't have to be just a cost; rather, they can be more profitable in the long term.

CHAPTER 3

DEAL FAIRLY AND ETHICALLY WITH SUPPLIERS, EMPLOYEES, AND CUSTOMERS

"The first step in the evolution of ethics is a sense of solidarity with other human beings."

—Albert Schweitzer

At first blush this practice may not seem to be connected directly to global sustainability, but in a way, it is foundational to all the others. Ethical commitments are necessary before you can make any other kinds of commitments, and if you aren't trustworthy, none of the benefits of the other practices described in this book will accrue to you or your business in any meaningful way.

Your reputation is your business's most precious asset. Without it, you are a pariah. No one who has any other options will want to work for you, and the employees you do have will come to work under a cloud of resentment, doing only the minimum amount of work they need to do to avoid being fired, and jumping ship at the first opportunity. Your customer base will give their business to your competition or simply do without the services you provide. And if you think the nature of your business makes you permanently indispensible to your customers, and that you have no serious competition, you'd better think again; just ask the owner of any disreputable taxi service how business has been in recent years. The iron grip of even the most powerful monopoly can endure only until the next technological breakthrough renders its business model obsolete.

As a conscious leader it is important to consider the impact of your decisions on all stakeholders. That includes employees, customers, and suppliers. They are all critical components of your success, and they are all connected to the ecosystem in which you operate. If you treat them with respect, they will respond in kind, and only in this atmosphere can your business—or any business—remain sustainable.

The Transparent World

I've mentioned this subject in passing twice already in this book, but at this point I'd like to discuss it in greater depth: the world of the twenty-first century is a transparent world in which unethical behavior is not so easily swept under the rug as it once was. If your company has been around for any significant length of time, chances are your Wikipedia page contains a subhead titled "Controversy" or "Criticism." If your last CEO was convicted of attempting to bribe a congressman, or if carelessness and corner-cutting caused a fire or an explosion that took hundreds of employees' lives, people will know. And they will talk. And tweet. And they will write articles that get shared and passed around on Facebook like mashed potatoes on Thanksgiving. The public doesn't quickly forget such betrayals of their trust, and nowadays a rundown of your ethical transgressions can be found in no more time than it takes to type the word *Yelp*.

Paul Polman of Unilever says, "We live in this age of increasing transparency. So we have more data coming out of our ears than we know what to do with, and . . . because of this transparency we're held to a higher standard of accountability. People will see now anywhere in the world how you treat your labor . . . People can see if you sell beef or horsemeat now, and we just don't want to [be caught selling them] horsemeat when we say it's beef. People want to know where the products [they buy] come from; people want to know how you treat your people."

Seth Goldman, co-founder and "TeaEo Emeritus" of Honest Tea, echoes this sentiment: "It's apparent that we're in this age of transparency, [and that] that's the expectation consumers have. So [they] feel a sense of entitlement. And when they feel a company isn't being transparent, it's [an] uphill sales proposition for [that] company. Consumers have a right to know what's in their product, how it's being made, and where it's coming from. Not every consumer digs that deep . . . some consumers just want to understand that the company is being transparent, and then that's almost enough in itself. [But] others really want to go much deeper . . . [b]ut if someone says, 'Hey, this is a company that's doing what it says it's doing,' sometimes that's enough. I can't think of any sector where consumers will say, 'I don't want to know how you're doing or what you're doing. I just want you to give me a product.'"

It's telling that Polman and Goldman both make such prominent use of the word *transparency* in their remarks. This transparency, the fishbowl in which we all must do business, makes it vital to cultivate a public image of trustworthiness. Consumers want to trust the companies they buy from, and a good business leader will make it his or her top priority to foster that trust.

Dave MacLennan of Cargill says, "I want Cargill to be known as the most trusted source of sustainable food and food ingredients in the world. Do the customers we do business with say, 'I trust Cargill because they're ethical, because they're focusing on sustainability'? That's how you know you're a successful company: if customers are choosing you because they trust you, and because of your ethical standards."

Polman explained to me how a company's reputation can have far-reaching financial implications by reducing risk: "If you lower the risk, you lower the cost of capital; if you lower the cost of capital, you have increased profitability, [which] ultimately will be translated into the share price. And there is increasing evidence that that is the case."

In light of all this, it's clear that a company's concern for its reputation should be a guiding principle. In a prepared statement about global sustainability, Tata shares its ambition "[to] be amongst the twenty-five most admired corporate and employer brands globally, with a market capitalisation comparable to the twenty-five most valuable companies in the world." The statement goes on to say that, "In keeping with that vision, Tata companies are building multinational businesses that seek to differentiate themselves through customer-centricity, innovation, *trustworthiness, and values-driven business operations* [emphasis, mine], while balancing the interests of diverse stakeholders, including customers, employees, financial stakeholders, value chain partners, and society at large."

Ethical Treatment of Employees

Ethical employee relations as a best practice for sustainability will be the subject of an entire chapter of this book (in fact, the very next chapter), so I won't go into excessive detail here. Suffice it to say that, as I noted at the beginning of this chapter, you owe it to your employees to treat them fairly and with respect. These are the people you depend on to keep your business running smoothly, and regardless of whether an employee is the district manager for all of New England or merely a cashier or janitor, everything he or she does matters.

If employees are terrorized by verbal abuse or incessant micromanagement, or if they are frequently lied to, they will become resentful. At a minimum, frustrated, resentful employees are liable to do substandard work or quit at the first opportunity . . . and if they are treated poorly enough, they may even be tempted to sabotage you or steal from you. These people give nearly half of their waking lives to you, and the loyalty you can buy merely by treating them with respect—and paying them a decent wage—is beyond price.

Ethical Treatment of Customers

> *"I need to take care of my customers. We are making ingredients for medicines, so I cannot say to a patient, "Are you still using the medicine? Well bad luck for you, because we don't make so much profit on that anymore, so we stopped making it. That would be irresponsible. Those kinds of things you cannot do."*
> —**Feike Sijbesma**, CEO, DSM

Some readers may recall Volkswagen's recent blunder, in which the company admitted to equipping eleven million of its cars with software designed to cheat emissions tests.[18] The consequences of this breach of consumer trust were catastrophic for Volkswagen: in 2015 the company posted its first quarterly loss in fifteen years,[19] after

18   Karl Russell et al., "How Volkswagen Is Grappling With Its Diesel Deception," *The New York Times*, March 24, 2016

19   Jack Ewing, "Volkswagen, Hit by Emissions Scandal, Posts Its First Loss in Years," *The New York Times*, October 28, 2015

losing 23 percent of its value overnight.[20] Since the scandal broke, Volkswagen has been forced to set aside over $7 billion to cover the costs of making the affected vehicles compliant with emissions laws, and that figure may yet climb as high as $9 or $10 billion. The company may face fines of up to $37,500 for each affected vehicle— which would come, approximately, to another $18 billion.[21] And that's just a brief summary of the penalties the company faces in the United States; it will also face government action in Europe and elsewhere around the world.

As chilling as it is to contemplate the immediate financial repercussions of Volkswagen's mistake, the longer-term damage to the automaker's reputation is apt to be more significant. In November of 2015, US sales of Volkswagen cars were down 25 percent from November of the previous year.[22] That's a signal from the company's customers, letting the company and the world know how they feel about being lied to. A 2015 survey conducted by research and consulting firm AutoPacific reveals that only 25 percent of Americans now have a favorable view of Volkswagen, down from 75 percent before the scandal.[23]

The lesson in this is clear: treating customers with respect means more than just greeting them with a smile when they walk into your store. It means dealing with them honestly and ethically, and working to earn their trust. At a minimum, this means not lying to them.

---

20 Naomi Kresge, Richard Weiss, "Volkswagen Drops 23% After Admitting Diesel Emissions Cheat," *Bloomberg*, September 21, 2015

21 Benjamin Zhang, "There's No Way Volkswagen Will Pay the US $18 Billion in Fines for Cheating on Emissions Tests," *Business Insider*, September 21, 2015

22 Kristen Korosec, "Volkswagen's U.S. Auto Sales Got Crushed in November," *Fortune*, December 1, 2015.

23 Deborah Grieb, "Volkswagen's Reputation Takes Big Hit with Vehicle Owners," AutoPacific website, October 1, 2015: http://www.autopacific.com/news-app/ story.248/title.volkswagen-s-reputation-takes-big-hit-with-vehicle-owners-autopacific-predicts-tough-road-ahead

Ethical Treatment of Suppliers

Unilever's Paul Polman: "The uniqueness of our model is that . . . we actually take co-responsibility [for] the total value chain. If you are in food, that means from farm to fork . . . taking co-responsibility for how the small-holder farmer can make a living. [There are] five hundred thousand small-holder farms [in the world, whose owners] barely can eat, themselves. So how can we provide assistance to those people? We take responsibility across the total value chain to try to solve that, and we put measures behind that . . . for example, by making all of our agriculturally based raw materials sustainable."

Like Dave MacLennan, and like many of the other CEOs profiled in this book, Polman understands that it would be unethical to take advantage of the disparity in economic power between his company and its suppliers. This subject will be discussed at greater length in chapter 5, which is about showing concern for the well-being of the communities in which you do business (especially in underdeveloped parts of the world). For now, however, it seems appropriate to single out two companies that have built their entire business models on this practice: Sustainable Harvest® and Honest Tea.

When I interviewed Sustainable Harvest® CEO David Griswold, he explained to me what his nearly twenty-year-old company (founded in 1997) does: "Essentially we're a specialty coffee importer operating as a social enterprise hybrid. We try to invest in farming communities and help small-holder subsistence farmers who are what we call *pre-commercial*. We help them learn how to compete in the global chain and become commercial. For us, this is reinvesting back in the supply chain. Over the last decade we've been among the largest importers of fair-trade organic coffee in North America; last year, sales were in excess of $50 million."

Sustainable Harvest® touts itself as a pioneer of what it calls the "Relationship Coffee Model," the object of which, according to the company's website, is "to establish greater transparency between farmers and roasters."[24] Let's take a moment to recall one of the overarching themes of this book—that global sustainability isn't mere flower-child idealism; it's an important concern for any business that wishes to remain profitable. Griswold's pride in last year's sales underscores this point, and he's entitled to be proud of his company's performance; revenue doubled between 2010 and 2011, and Sustainable Harvest® has continued to grow since then.[25]

Seth Goldman's company, Honest Tea, says in the mission statement on its website, "We strive to grow our business with the same honesty and integrity we use to craft our products, with sustainability and great taste for all." Elsewhere on the same page, we learn about the effort the company puts into earning and keeping its Fair Trade certification: "In 2014 we paid $200,124 back to our tea- and sugar-sourcing communities in the form of fair-trade premiums. These funds have helped to establish improved farming, healthcare, and education initiatives." Scrolling down, we find videos detailing Honest Tea's commitment to fair-trade sourcing for its tea leaves, sugar, and other ingredients, and we learn how a portion of each purchase is returned to the communities in which these ingredients are grown, enabling them to make improvements in both their farming methods and their day-to-day lives.

Ethical Treatment of Investors and Other Stakeholders

When ethical behavior becomes a matter of habit, one finds that it's no longer necessary to ponder too deeply how one should conduct dealings with other people, whether in one's personal life or in any aspect of business. When it comes to ethical dealing with investors, of course, this principle is not just a matter of moral intuition, but also a matter of law.

---

24   http://www.sustainableharvest.com/about/

25   Lee van der Voo, "Sustainable Harvest Delivers Profit with Purpose," *Portland Business Journal*, May 7, 2012: http://www.bizjournals.com/portland/blog/sbo/2012/03/sustainable-harvest-delivers-profit.html

Despite lawmakers' best intentions, however, the reach of the law cannot be all encompassing. There are many unethical ways of doing business with investors, and many of these are perfectly legal. One important ethical consideration, especially for a company that is serious about making a commitment to support global sustainability, is whether the company's investors understand what that commitment may entail, e.g., lower quarterly returns, or sometimes even the sacrifice of significant long-term profit because the company eschews unethical or unsustainable business practices. While it might be perfectly legal to downplay these commitments, it would not be ethical to take money from investors who might be unaware of them, or who might fail to grasp their implications.

DSM's Feike Sijbesma is sensitive to this responsibility.

"Increasingly, shareholders understand this, because we are pretty vocal about what we want to be. This vision attracts investors who appreciate our intention to create value for all stakeholders, including shareholders."

CEO compensation is also an ethical consideration, although many executives might prefer not to think so. Tom Szaky is the founder and CEO of TerraCycle, a manufacturing company that makes its goods by "recycling the non-recyclable."

Szaky explained to me why he doesn't personally enrich himself at the expense of TerraCycle's stakeholders: "The way we perceive profit at TerraCycle . . . we are formally a for-profit organization . . . but we have set up a dynamic where we do not *focus* on profit . . . The difference between my salary as the highest paid individual and the lowest is [a factor of seven]. Ask the same question of some . . . other companies . . . and see what the answer may be."

Szaky is right to take pride in the manner in which he is compensated. There is no law prohibiting him from demanding a salary three hundred times greater than that of the average employee at his company—and many CEOs do just that. Earnings for CEOs have tripled in the last twenty years, and increased tenfold over the last thirty years. The ratio of top executive pay to that of the average Joe is 303 to 1—up from 20 to 1 in 1965.[26] This is unethical—grotesque, even—and as a society, we should demand more from our business leaders.

Key Takeaways

1. Your reputation is your business's most precious asset.
2. We live in a transparent world in which scandals cannot easily be swept under the rug.
3. You owe it to your employees to treat them fairly and with respect, and if you do so, they will repay you with loyalty, which is priceless.
4. Never lie to your investors.
5. Never, *ever* lie to your customers.

---

26 Paul Hodgson, "Top CEOs Make More Than 300 Times the Average Worker," *Fortune*, June 22, 2015

CHAPTER 4

BE CONCERNED ABOUT YOUR EMPLOYEES' MOTIVATION AND WELL-BEING

"I have always believed that the way you treat your employees is the way they will treat your customers, and that people flourish when they are praised."

—**Richard Branson**, founder, Virgin Group

"Employee loyalty begins with employer loyalty. Your employees should know that if they do the job they were hired to do with a reasonable amount of competence and efficiency, you will support them."

—**Harvey Mackay**, best-selling author of
Swim with the Sharks without Being Eaten Alive

Employees are the lifeblood of any organization. If they are not supported and taken care of, the organization will not be sustainable. Few business concerns are more important than your employees' health, safety, engagement—and *motivation*.

This chapter is about the *people* part of the triple-bottom-line equation, and the importance of inspiring and empowering the people who work for you. Employees who feel secure in their jobs, and who feel respected and trusted, will go to surprising lengths to earn and keep their employers' respect.

Most people are forever looking for satisfaction and meaning in their lives. We need to feel that we are valuable members of the societies in which we live, and that the contributions we make to those societies *matter*. Therefore, when we know we have done good work—and when our satisfaction in a job well done is validated with praise, encouragement, and the opportunity to take on more challenging responsibilities—our brains are flooded with a chemical called *dopamine*.

Dopamine is part of the brain's reward system, which serves to reward and reinforce desirable behavior, and the pleasure we derive from this dopamine rush is addictive. The upshot of all this, of course, is that if we are recognized and rewarded for our good work, we will redouble our efforts to continue to earn such recognition.

In short, happy employees are more productive employees. There is no worse distraction in the workplace than perpetual anxiety. Employees who understand themselves to be valued members of a team are more confident and relaxed, and therefore, more innovative and energetic. Such employees invariably provide better customer service, which results in happier customers—which leads to more business and higher profits.

A Historical Perspective on Employee Well-Being

Lest you write this off as mere theory, I'd like to illustrate my point with a historical example: automaker Henry Ford.

Ford was a controversial figure in his own time, and his legacy is fraught even today. On one hand, his embrace of assembly-line production enabled his company to produce cars that the average American could afford, thereby transforming the automobile from a rich man's plaything into a tool for the common man. On the other hand, he was an open anti-Semite who continued to do business with Nazi Germany until America's entry into World War II forced him to stop.

Notwithstanding Ford's character and his prejudices, however, he was indisputably a business visionary who understood that his employees' well-being was integral to the building of his empire—and the results he achieved with this understanding speak for themselves.

Ford was an early adopter of a business practice that would eventually become known as "welfare capitalism," or "industrial paternalism." The idea behind this concept, essentially, was that businesses prosper by paying higher wages and offering benefits to their employees. Ford felt that efficiency depended on a company's ability to retain the brightest and most dedicated workers, and that it was unacceptable to have to hire three hundred men each year to fill a hundred jobs.

Competitive wages were the heart of this strategy, so in 1914, Ford began offering a then-unheard-of five dollars per day to his employees— effectively doubling the salaries of most of his assembly-line workers. The results of this move materialized almost immediately: the best mechanics in Detroit beat a path to his door, and his competitors were forced to offer comparable wages or risk losing their most talented people.

Another result of this wage increase was that Ford employees could now afford to buy the cars they made, and this contributed to a general growth in the regional economy. More important to our discussion here, however, is the effect of this revolution on Henry Ford himself, and on his company: at the time of his death, Ford was a multibillionaire, and today his company is a colossus; it was the ninth-ranked American company on *Fortune*'s 2015 Fortune 500 list,[27] with record-setting pretax profits in excess of $10 billion.[28]

Safety

The consequences of inattention to worker safety can be devastating. DSM CEO Feike Sijbesma told me a little about his company's history: "Over time we sold all our bulk chemical activities and became the life-sciences and materials-sciences company we are today. We had two big explosions in the seventies, when we were still a petrochemical company—one in the UK, and one in the Netherlands. Lives were lost, and we said, 'This is unacceptable. We need to have responsible care. We need to take care of safety. And since the seventies, safety has been expanded—not only for our people, but also for the people around our plants.'"

Dave MacLennan of Cargill told me quite a bit about his company's commitment to safety: "We've established specific sustainability standards for the farmer coops from whom we buy cocoa. [This includes] personal safety concerns, such as asking them to use sticks rather than machetes to crack open cocoa pods. They've got these pods, which are about the size of, maybe, half a volleyball, and traditionally, they'll split them open with a machete. And then they take the cocoa beans and they dry them on a big banana leaf. And we've said, 'We don't want you to use the machetes; we want you using these sticks because it's safer.'

"And so if we certify that a coop or a cocoa farm has met our standards of sustainability, which is part of the Cargill Cocoa Promise, we pay them a premium for their cocoa beans."[29]

---

27 http://fortune.com/fortune500/
28 https://media.ford.com/content/dam/fordmedia/North%20America/US/2016/01/28/4qfinancials.pdf
29 The Cargill Cocoa Promise, from Cargill's website: "Our aim is to accelerate progress towards a transparent global cocoa supply chain, enable farmers and their communities to achieve better incomes and living standards, and deliver a sustainable supply of cocoa and chocolate products."

MacLennan is also a keen observer of the examples set by others who came before him: "Paul O'Neill, a CEO of Alcoa back in the '90s, made safety his mantra, and he substantially increased the equity market capitalization of Alcoa in part by focusing on safety. His belief—and I share that belief—was that it would follow through to everything else that you do: your commitment to process, your commitment to excellence, and your commitment to your employees. And their safety will inspire them."

Wages and Incentives

We've already made the point that higher wages attract more talented, dedicated employees; the example of Ford Motor Company makes this case better than most. Even today, a great many companies understand the wisdom of Henry Ford's approach. Pacific Seafood Group gives a total of 20 percent of its profits back to its team members; up to 10 percent goes into their profit-sharing plan and 10 percent goes toward incentives.

"We give 20 percent of our profits back to our team members in two parts," Pacific Seafood CEO Frank Dulcich told me. "Up to 10 percent goes into their profit-sharing plan, and the other 10 percent goes into incentives. Every one of our team members is incentivized on what they can control operationally or can influence. Most of the ideas for how we process, handle, and prepare fish [i.e., how Pacific Seafood contributes to global sustainability by drastically reducing food waste, a topic we'll get into in chapter 7] have really come from team members doing their jobs and looking at how we can continually improve."

Dulcich's comments underscore not just the importance of paying people well, but also the importance of making them feel valued and important. This speaks to the next aspect of employee well-being that we'll cover: *engagement*.

Engagement and Communication

Barrett Values Centre is a management consulting firm whose website advertises "powerful metrics that enable leaders to measure and manage the cultures of their organisations, and the leadership development needs of their managers and leaders." Phil Clothier is Barrett's CEO, and he told me one of the firm's success stories:

"I'm not going to tell you the name of the company, but it's a global firm with offices in 147 nations. Each year the whole firm completes an employee-engagement study. The scores for one of the nations had typically been around 65 percent, meaning that their people were 65 percent engaged.

"I'm simplifying a little bit, but they used Barrett's leadership values assessment, and in the course of one year, the employee-engagement score went up in that country from 65 percent to 87 percent. As we say all the time, it's the consciousness of the leaders that creates the culture of the organization. And because of the work they did, their employees felt like, *I want to go to work today. This is much more fun here. And this is working for me.* And the global board saw this shift happen in this one nation and said, 'What the hell's going on? How did you achieve that level of miracle?' And that program is now being rolled out globally based on that one shift from 65 percent to 87 percent in one year. They looked into it and said, 'Well, what's actually happening on the ground [demonstrates] the effectiveness of happy employees, happy customers, and the positive impact it's having on our business.'"

As Clothier says, "It's the consciousness of the leaders that creates the culture of the organization." If your company is saddled with disengaged employees, chances are you need look no further than the nearest mirror to find the source of the problem. Ask yourself, "What have I done to inspire these people? What have I done to make them care about this company as much as I do?"

Cargill's Dave MacLennan takes employee engagement very seriously, and like Clothier and his clients, he studies and measures it among his employees.

"We conduct an employee-engagement survey about every eighteen months to two years. We go to the entire organization and say, 'Tell us how we're doing. Are you engaged? Are you excited about working here? Are you referring others to come to Cargill? How often do you think about leaving?' And [the answers to these questions tell us whether or not] our employees believe in the direction of the company and what we're doing."

MacLennan's (and Cargill's) interest in employee job satisfaction is indicative of his firm grasp of the importance of *communication*. If employees are kept in the dark about the company's direction, its general financial health, or any other matter that directly affects them, morale can suffer, and rumors can begin to spread throughout the company. This, in turn, makes employees jittery and anxious—and as I said earlier, there is no worse distraction in the workplace than anxiety.

Of course, one of the primary sources of employee anxiety is fear of losing one's job. This kind of fear mustn't be allowed to spread. One way to keep such fears at bay is to avoid being in the habit of letting people go unless it's absolutely necessary.

Although many companies hire outside consultants to measure employee engagement, and many others communicate with employees by conducting extensive in-house surveys, keeping open lines of communication between management and lower-level employees doesn't need to be difficult or complicated.

Honest Tea's Seth Goldman told me how his company does it: "We have an e-mail newsletter called *Afternoon Tea*, which we send out to all our employees two times a week. It's our almost-daily update on what the company's up to. Whether we have a meeting with a particular supplier or we were recognized for a particular association with a nonprofit, we'll share that information with all the employees."

> *"One of the most gratifying things for me is the employee owner meeting I do every year. I let our folks know what we're up to and how we're doing."*
> —**Mike Sangiacomo**, CEO, Recology

In the previous section I discussed the importance of paying fair, competitive wages. Paying your employees well is essential, but it's not enough. Your employees need to feel that they're being treated fairly, and that what they're paid is commensurate with what others in the company—and elsewhere in your industry—are being paid for comparable work. For reasons that I trust are obvious, this is crucial to employee engagement.

Salesforce explained to me how vital they feel that sense of fairness is to employee morale: "We believe in equal rights for our employees. We recently looked at every single one of our female employees' salaries, and we adjusted it against all of our male employees' salaries. This was a $3 million investment in combatting inequality and living our values."

In sum, an employee's engagement—his willingness and ability to devote 100 percent of his attention to his job at all times, his loyalty, and his emotional stake in your company—depends on a number of factors: a sense that his job is secure, a sense that management communicates with him and cares about his opinion, and his feeling that he is being treated fairly and paid fairly for the time and effort he invests.

I'll let Unilever's Paul Polman have the last word on employee engagement.

"What drives people in motivation besides the minimum salary that we all need? Obviously, people want good education, they want safety, and they want air they can breathe, water they can drink.

"In a company, that is not different. You need to pay people competitively—and we do that—but then people want to learn, they want to develop, they want to belong, and they want to be respected, and these are all human needs that are far more important than bonuses."

Opportunity

Mike Sangiacomo is the CEO of Recology, a San Francisco-based waste-management company that works to find profitable uses for the waste and trash it collects, rather than simply dumping it into landfills or incinerators (as you've no doubt guessed already, you'll learn more about Recology in forthcoming chapters). Since its founding in 1986, the company has been 100 percent employee-owned through its Employee Stock Ownership Plan (ESOP), with no outside investors.

I asked Sangiacomo about Recology's employee ownership, and what it means to him and his employees. This is what he told me:

"Being employee-owned, to me, is hugely important. Our management team makes fair compensation levels, but I've been in the ESOP since it started and I have the biggest account in our ESOP plan, and that represents about one third of one percent of the company. That's not enough to make anybody rich, but we made a determination that it is better for us in the long term, and better for our company and our community, that we share what we do with everybody who works here. It doesn't matter what job someone has; he or she participates in the ESOP.

"We have taken a lot of people out of the city's housing projects and turned them into people who used to drive to work in old junkers and [now own] some pretty nice cars. We've turned a lot of them into the homeowners that they never imagined in their lives that they ever could possibly be. I think all that is good for the environment in that it spreads the wealth around, and I think we've done a lot to eliminate poverty with the people. Not everybody who came to work here out of housing projects made it, but those who got it said, 'Yes, I want to take advantage of a way out,' and it's worked."

The lesson here is obvious: Recology is a hugely successful business, in part because all its employees have a stake in the company's success.

> *"We're 70 percent full-time, which is unusual in the supermarket business, which is typically 30 percent full-time. And we have made Fortune's list of the 100 Best Companies to Work For® seventeen years in a row. Our guy that's running our busy store in New York started out as a part-time janitor in the stores. The opportunity we have in our company is pretty amazing."*
> —**Walter Robb**, co-CEO, Whole Foods Market

Everyone needs and wants opportunities to succeed in life. That opportunity needn't necessarily take the form of part ownership in the company one works for; for many people, it's enough simply to work for a company that promotes from within whenever possible—for a company that is willing to train lower-level employees for better jobs within the company. Opportunity to advance, or opportunity to own some of the fruits of one's labor—either of these can be enough to give a worker a reason to come to work in the morning fully engaged and determined to give his or her best.

"I strongly believe that there should be more sharing of wealth in companies among the people who actually do the work," says Sangiacomo. "So we're weird; we're different."

Should your company also consider trying something different?

Key Takeaways

1. High wages enable a company to attract and retain the brightest and most dedicated workers.

2. The consequences of inattention to safety can be devastating.

3. Engagement is a measure of the degree to which employees believe in the company's mission.

4. Communication is important to company morale.

5. Fairness is *critical* to company morale.

CHAPTER 5

SUPPORT THE WELL-BEING OF THE COMMUNITIES WHERE YOU DO BUSINESS

"It is every man's obligation to put back into the world at least the equivalent of what he takes out of it."
—Albert Einstein

Most businesses of any significant size have concerns in a variety of places around the country and around the world. A company whose corporate headquarters is located in Los Angeles may have branch offices in New York and London; factories in Singapore; distribution facilities in Texas, Thailand, and Bangladesh; warehouses in Nevada and Taipei, and so forth. The supply chains of such companies may extend all over the world, reaching into remote, poverty-stricken parts of Africa, Asia, or South America. Many companies deal in goods that can only be produced in certain climates—coffee, for example—or they outsource labor to other countries because it is cheaper.

Whatever your reasons for doing any kind of business in any community, whether it is a small factory town in Indiana or a remote cocoa-farming village in Ecuador, it is a moral imperative that you keep in mind the effect of your operations on the people who live there. In many cases, these people will constitute your labor pool; in other cases, they will be mere innocent bystanders—like the residents of Irwindale, California, whose lives were made unbearable for months by the noxious emissions of the Sriracha plant that began operating there in 2011.[30] The city of Irwindale eventually sued Huy Fong Foods, which makes Sriracha, and the result of the whole affair was an avalanche of bad publicity for the company—and a general public perception that its owner, David Tran, was indifferent to the discomfort caused by his operation.

Pollution is one of the more serious considerations affecting a company's relationship to its host community, but there are others—economic concerns, for example. If a company grows large enough, the towns in which its offices or factories are located may become economically dependent on it. Michael Moore's 1989 documentary film *Roger & Me* famously documented such a case; the film depicts the suffering in Flint, Michigan, following General Motors' closure of a number of plants there and the resultant loss of some thirty thousand jobs. The effect of this bad publicity on GM? A loss of market share to add to its already lengthy list of woes.

---

30   Ian Lovett, "Sriracha Factory Irritates Some California Noses, but Entices Politicians," The *New York Times*, May 13, 2014

There's a lesson to be learned from the misfortunes of both GM and Huy Fong Foods: it pays to be concerned about the welfare of people who are directly affected by your business operations.

The Value of Giving Back

Giving back to the communities that supply you with labor and raw materials isn't just a matter of ethics or public relations; it's also a wise business practice to adopt for its own sake. In a sense, it is an outgrowth of the practice we discussed in chapter 2, "Practice Long-Term Thinking." Taking care of the people who live and work in your company's shadow ensures the long-term sustainability of your supply chain and improves the quality of the talent pool that may someday produce your best and brightest employees. Perhaps more important, it ensures that in the long term, you will be *allowed to continue* to do business in these communities.

Ann Sherry and Carnival Australia—
"You Need Them to Want You to Come."

Ann Sherry has been CEO of Carnival Australia since 2007. Prior to that, she enjoyed a colorful career that included a stint as First Assistant Secretary of the Office of the Status of Women in Canberra, Australia, from 1992 to 1994. In that position, she was responsible for advising the prime minister on how to improve the status of women in Australia, and she represented the Australian government in the United Nations on matters connected to women's rights and human rights.

Carnival Australia is a cruise ship operator with destinations in remote areas of the Pacific Ocean. Many of these destinations are small countries with underdeveloped economies—indeed, some of these societies do not have any cash economy at all. When I spoke to Ms. Sherry, she explained to me how Carnival concerns itself with the well-being of the people who inhabit these places, and why it is necessary for them to do so.

"To really be sustainable in a business like ours, you need partnerships with the places you go because you need them to *want* you to come. If they don't want us to come, they can lock us out in a nanosecond. So, if the chief of an island we go to in the Pacific were to wake up one morning and go, *We get nothing from this; they're not coming ever again,* we'd be thrown into complete chaos.

"So, if you think about the consequences of people not wanting you to come, then you've got to think about how you create the opportunity we create by coming, not just for us—because I can define *that* very clearly—but for them. And so that's led us to rethink the way we engage with the communities we go to in the Pacific."

In other words, the islanders must benefit economically from Carnival's presence, or the business is endangered.

"You have to engage with people. We say, 'OK, we bring people to you. What do you need to make that work for you?' And they can articulate it very clearly; they say, 'Well, we need help to set up a market. We need to know what people want to buy because we don't know. And we need help to harness our local resources, and maybe to involve some of the communities around us because we live on a big island, and if only one village gets benefits, then that creates problems on the island.' 'OK,' we say.

"Then we work with the local community. We say, 'Let's get a committee together to talk about how you could make something more out of this. And someone always emerges from the community who's got a bit of entrepreneurial spirit, and those people are natural leaders.

"Anyway, so we work with them to say all right, every time the ship comes, maybe you can gather thirty people who have something to sell. Maybe you could go out and catch fresh seafood and you could offer that as lunch. And in one case, they came back to us then and said, 'Why don't we take people out to catch fish with us?' 'Fine,' we said, 'what a great idea.' And they said, 'Oh, but we've only got these dugout canoes.' And we looked at these and thought maybe we don't want people floating around the Pacific in a dugout canoe. So we bought some more stable kayaks [so that the islanders] could use them to run short tours, take people out fishing, and give them an experience. And that gives them real cash, so now they've started to do more work in their community that once they couldn't afford—putting solar panels on, and things like that."

By working in this way with the people whose homes serve as the backdrop for Carnival's customers' vacations, Sherry builds an economic relationship between them and her company. And, of course, this cooperation serves Carnival's interests by providing its customers with an authentic local experience.

Social License to Operate

Ann Sherry's work with local populations is a perfect example of a company seeking and acquiring *social license*, or *social license to operate*.[31] This term generally refers to a community's acceptance or approval of a project or a company's ongoing presence. Unlike regulatory license (which depends on government), social license is informal, being based on the feelings of a community. This informality can make it difficult to determine whether social license has been granted, and a company that is not monitoring its relationship with the local community may be caught unawares if its social license to operate has been revoked (as happened to Huy Fong Foods in Irwindale).

There are varying degrees to which social license may be granted: mere absence of opposition constitutes a kind of license—albeit a

31 Brian F. Yates and Celesa L. Horvath, *Social License to Operate: How to Get It, and How to Keep It*, Pacific Energy Summit Working Paper, available for download at http://www.nbr.org

fragile one—whereas some communities grant certain businesses overwhelming license to operate (consider the goodwill Carnival has earned from the Pacific islanders who welcome Carnival's customers into their communities).

Social license is not irrevocable; it can be diminished or even lost due to unforeseen events or due to a company's actions. This makes it *conditional*, a trait it shares to some degree with regulatory license (which a government can and will revoke in response to violations of laws or regulations). This is important to understand, as more and more companies are beginning to understand that social license to operate is necessary for a company that wishes to avoid costly problems further down the road.

In sum, social license is important to companies because it confers legitimacy upon a company's presence in a community. This helps to minimize the risk of costly opposition to company projects, and it serves to safeguard a company's reputation if something goes wrong (e.g., environmental disasters, unexpectedly necessary layoffs, etc.). Social license can be increased by operating with greater concern for community and environmental well-being (Dow Chemical did this in Thailand in the 1980s, as we will learn later in this chapter).

Ethical Sources—Human Rights across the Supply Chain

When I refer to "the communities where you do business," I'm not just referring to places where you visibly show up (in the way that a Carnival Cruise ship shows up on the shore of a Pacific island, for example). Depending on what business you're in, your company can affect the lives of people you never directly interact with—via your supply chain.

French luxury-goods company Kering is just such an entity. As the parent or part owner of a wide variety of luxury and lifestyle brands—including Gucci, Brioni, PUMA, Boucheron, and many others—Kering sources material from all over the globe to make clothing, leather goods, and jewelry. Kering's chairman and CEO, François-Henri Pinault, explained to me why it's important for Kering to able to obtain its materials ethically.

"When you start to be really active in the sustainability field, your company comes back to you and says, 'OK, fine, we know how to do it in a proper way, but it costs more, so we will have to accept less profits.' And I say it's not [enough] just to find solutions; it's also [necessary] to make sure that sustainable solutions are economically viable, and private corporations have a role in that.

"I will give you an example that we achieved on ethical gold.[32] Three years ago, we decided to explore sourcing our gold from ethical, fair-mined gold suppliers, and, of course, the first response from my team was to say it would cost us 20 percent more than the regular gold. So we said, OK, let's find a way to work with those mines to reuse that price difference to make sure that it's a sustainable practice over time. And after two years, we were able to bring the price difference from 20 percent to less than 1 percent. And now we are moving forward, and within probably two years from now, 100 percent of our gold will be ethical gold."

By committing to ethical gold, Pinault and Kering are aligning themselves with the UN's global Sustainable Development Goals—specifically, Goal 16: "Promote just, peaceful, and inclusive societies . . ."[33]

Honest Tea takes their responsibility for human rights seriously too, and CEO Seth Goldman described to me how that subject is tied to considerations like wages. "Because we source all our tea leaves from Fair Trade Certified™ communities, it also means that the working conditions

---

32 Gold mining is difficult, dangerous labor. Millions of gold miners are exploited by unscrupulous middlemen who pay them starvation-level wages, and many of these workers are children or slaves. "Ethical gold" is gold that is obtained from sources that use verifiable, transparent supply chains in order to circumvent this problem.

33 http://www.undp.org/content/undp/en/home/sdgoverview/post-2015-development-agenda/goal-16.html

[need to be looked at]. This is where addressing poverty comes in; we are looking at the working conditions, making sure there's no child labor or prison labor. But we're also looking at the wages paid to the workers."

Fair Trade

Because of Honest Tea's values—its Guiding Principles—Fair Trade certification is of utmost importance to them. The company's commitment to Fair Trade is inseparable from its brand identity. I said in chapter 3 that it is unethical for a company to take advantage of the disparity in economic power between itself and its suppliers. The growth in popularity of Fair Trade coffee over the last decade is ample testimony that consumers around the world increasingly share this feeling.

The term *fair trade* means pretty much what it sounds like it means: Wikipedia defines it as "a social movement whose stated goal is to help producers in developing countries achieve better trading conditions and to promote sustainability [and whose members] advocate the payment of higher prices to exporters." Third-party certification organizations like Fair Trade USA work to ensure that certified companies abide by their standards, and "to guarantee that the farmers and workers producing Fair Trade Certified™ goods are paid fair prices and wages, [and] work in safe conditions . . ."[34]

For some companies, Fair Trade certification is a core element of their business model. Coffee importer Sustainable Harvest® works hard to educate small-holder farmers about their place in the supply chain, and to help them grow.

CEO David Griswold says, "If we can train those people to be effective business leaders, we can create sustainability."

Honest Tea is another such company, and Seth Goldman told me about Honest Tea's investment in earning their Fair Trade certification: "We're selling organic tea, and we have to find high-quality tea that

---

34 Fair Trade USA website: http://fairtradeusa.org/about-fair-trade-usa/who-we-are

tastes great. And once we've identified it, if possible, we'll try to visit the garden, or some representative [will do so] on our behalf; that representative would be either a broker we work with or a representative from Fair Trade USA or their network. So in order to gain the certifications, we have to have people on the ground. We've also done this with Fair Trade sugar.

"I can't name an occasion when we've ever decided to go for something cheaper. Every time we've made a decision concerning our ingredients—and we started with most of the conventional nonorganic ingredients—we've moved to organic. And then we moved to Fair Trade. And in each case, when we make that decision, we're increasing our cost and also increasing the complexity and challenge of our supply chain. But part of what we've done at the same time is also keeping the depth of our brand. The value of our brand. The power of our brand."

Sustainable Harvest®

Because the focus of this chapter is the practice of supporting the well-being of the communities where you do business, I want to single out Sustainable Harvest® for special attention. For this company, this practice is more than just an aspect of how they conduct themselves as corporate citizens; it is their entire raison d'être. I'll let CEO David Griswold tell you more:

"I started in 1990, so it was very early on that I was down in Mexico working with Campesino farmers and realizing how disconnected they are from the supply chain. And there was a moment of epiphany when I knew I would go into sustainable coffee.

"Just to give you context, I first started in coffee in 1989 or 1990, when the Berlin Wall was falling. So the coffee quotas that had been in place for decades—that kept prices at a certain level of livable wage—had all collapsed.

"And so I was in Mexico as a volunteer, trying to figure out how I could be a helpful volunteer before I went off to business school. And coffee was in this free-fall of prices, going from about $1.20 down to, eventually, about forty-eight cents. I saw that the farmers had no idea whom to even argue against, because it was all liberalization of the market. There was no longer a government intervention in the market, and no more agricultural support. Everything had been sort of dismantled all at once.

"Watching all of that, I remember sitting in the office in Mexico City where I would go, and I vividly remember, a guy named Pedro came in. He had come from about a seven-hour bus ride from northern Mexico, where he had brought in some coffee beans in parchment, which is that peanut-like shell that covers the green coffee beans that you roast.

"And he came in and he said—we were speaking in Spanish—'I heard you're going to help us sell our beans.' And I thought, *My gosh, I've been in this for about two or three months and I know very little about coffee.* But I did know that he couldn't take the coffee and parchment beans and send it up to a broker or trading house, and that he didn't realize the importance of that very minimal step. And it struck me how disconnected these farmers were from sustaining their future and being part of the global supply chain.

"And so I didn't really give Pedro a good answer that day, but he had given me the answer for the rest of my life. I spent the next twenty-five years trying to build a company that helps those people who need support to participate in global supply chains, especially the people who are managing rural farmer organizations, who don't get a lot of support. If we can train those people to be effective business leaders, we can create sustainability.

"I felt that quality of coffee really went hand in hand with the quality of life for farmers who could take care of their farms. We had to get out of this conundrum of prices that were below cost of production. So with that in mind, when things like fair trade or organic or any of the certifications that paid higher prices came around, I was always the first to get on board and promote that.

"Everybody has their costs and their challenges, and we have to figure out how to maximize the profitability of all parts of the supply chain so everybody feels like there is something. So it's not a zero-sum game, which I think it often is now.

"Climate change in coffee is a very big issue. Obviously, agriculture gets hit with climate-change issues sooner than almost anything else. We may not pay attention to landslides in Columbia or floods in Peru or whatever, but you certainly hear about it when you're trying to ship containers of coffee and get trucks out and things like that.

"But the most specific example I can give of climate change affecting coffee was the leaf rust that obliterated parts of Central America a couple of years ago. Coffee-leaf rust is a fungus that spreads in warmer climates, and it was reaching high-altitude areas that had never been hit before. They called it *la roya*, 'the rust.' So our staff was on the ground early, visiting farms in Central America, and they said, 'Hey, there's something really wrong. All the leaves are falling off the trees and they've got all these orange spots. Eventually, it took out 30 to 40 percent of their production in certain parts of Central America, and caused a lot of migration into the US—people leaving coffee farms in places like El Salvador or Guatemala.

"It was not clear what the problem was, but we knew that we had to get to our farmer groups with information about this disease—what is it and what can you do about it. Please don't spray because you're organic and you'll lose your organic certification for at least three years. And there was nothing being done. Nothing would work for organic coffee farmers, and that's a huge problem because maybe 85 percent of our business is organic.

"So I mobilized. I called my roaster partners, people I sell the coffee to and said here's the problem, and we're putting together a training video. We don't have the expertise here, but we know that in certain parts of Central America and Guatemala and El Salvador and Honduras and Columbia there are experts. So let's go and film them and then we will get all of our suppliers a video that explains what coffee rust is, and what you can do. And then we ran a conference shortly thereafter and we brought in all the experts."

Industrial Paternalism—A Heavy Responsibility

In the last chapter I talked a bit about Henry Ford's "industrial paternalism." And earlier in this chapter I mentioned another Detroit-area auto giant, General Motors, and its failure to sustain the livelihoods of thirty thousand of its employees. A large enough company can dominate the economy of any community in which it does business, and we can see in Detroit today the consequences that arise when the patronage of such a company or industry is withdrawn. This makes it ethically important for any such business to consider the effects of business decisions on dependent communities.

Pacific Seafood's Frank Dulcich understands this well. His company employs thirty-five hundred people year round, and that number goes up by about fifteen hundred during the company's busy season. The coastal fishing communities that depend on Pacific Seafood for their livelihoods are never far from his thoughts.

"It's our social responsibility," he says. "It's part of our core philosophy, and our standards of how we have to act as a steward and a good corporate citizen in these communities. There are a number of these small coastal communities, and we'll employ two to three hundred people [in each of them]. And without that sustainable marine resource, these communities would be in dire straits."

Whole Foods co-CEO Walter Robb is mindful of the need in many underserved communities for supermarkets like his. Poor neighborhoods in many major cities are "food deserts," where supermarkets are scarce.

In such a community, the appearance of a store like Whole Foods can be transformational, not just by providing residents with a place to buy groceries, but also by providing employment opportunities.

"We take the responsibility of being a good employer and creating jobs," Robb told me. "And at the end of the day, particularly in a city like Detroit, it's not even so much about the food as it is about the jobs and the economic opportunity the store represents. So we're building stores in underserved communities in Detroit and New Orleans, and on the South Side of Chicago in Englewood and in Newark [New Jersey], and then we're working on a couple of others. In the end, that direct investment into a community creates jobs—whether it's for team members or for the suppliers whom we encourage to get started and grow their businesses to support the store. This is what happened in Detroit, where now we have [created] close to two hundred jobs. In Englewood, on the South Side of Chicago, there is an average per capita income of $21,000. We will create a hundred jobs when that store opens, and we will create twenty-five new suppliers. And those are meaningful, tangible, direct economic impacts or contributions toward supporting the community."

TOMS Shoes, a company that built its success on a philanthropic business model, is similarly concerned with job creation.

Founder Blake Mycoskie says, "I think one of our big goals was to take more of our manufacturing of our Giving Shoes to the communities in the countries that we were giving in, because we knew that this would create jobs in these communities, which is super important, and it would also decrease the cost in time and carbon footprint of shipping shoes around the world. And we've seen a huge impact; these communities are telling us about the impact, not just in terms of job creation, but also in how much better it is not to have to ship the shoes to get them to the people who need them the most. We're in about seventy countries right now."

Investing in Healthy, Stable Communities

Employment isn't the only benefit TOMS Shoes brings to the poor countries where it has a presence. Mycoskie's initial inspiration for his "one for one" giving program, and for his company's business model, came from the poverty he saw in underdeveloped countries.

"TOMS started with a very simple need. While traveling in Argentina, I saw kids without shoes who weren't going to school because they didn't have the proper uniforms—and that included shoes, which was the most expensive part of the uniform.

"I didn't really have a lot of thoughts about these macro sustainability issues or the global goals when I started; I just wanted to help kids get shoes so they could go to school. And as we've grown TOMS, we've learned a lot. Our shoes aren't just used for people who go to school; they're used to really help provide better health. A lot of diseases, like hookworm, are contracted through the feet, and children who don't have shoes contract these at a much, much higher rate than those who do.

"Our giving goes beyond shoes, supporting programs like vaccinations and incentives to get vaccinated. Some of our giving partners have started to use the shoes as a way to entice mothers to bring their kids in to get vaccinations. We've also focused on local manufacturing and creating jobs, and on reducing our carbon footprint in the shipping of shoes.

"So up until about three years ago, we made all of our shoes in Asia, and now 40 percent of the shoes that we give are made in the countries we give in; so, we're making shoes in Haiti; we're making shoes in Kenya; we're making shoes in India, Ethiopia, and Mexico. And the great thing about that is not only are we creating jobs, but now we're not shipping shoes all the way across the world; we make them right there and then give them in those countries."

Shoes aren't the only benefit TOMS Shoes brings to these places—they also conduct eye exams.

"The goal is to help children not only get the right uniform and be in school, but also to thrive in school. And so we do a lot of eye screening exams domestically and internationally to help children who are having trouble seeing the chalkboard in class. This is often misdiagnosed as a learning disability, when really, they just have problems with their eyesight. So both our shoe program and our eyesight program, whether it's surgeries or prescription glasses, are ultimately benefiting a child's ability to be in school and learn in the best way they can."

Honest Tea contributes to similar eye-care programs in Assam, India.

Seth Goldman told me why they do this: "Two years ago, we invested in eye care in the community in Assam because they didn't have any access to eye care. And when we can make these types of investments that help to develop long-term economic self-sufficiency in these communities, that's a way to address poverty. Now, I don't want to sound like we're totally altruistic; these are also smart investments in our supply chain. So there's very little downside to making these types of investments."

Public approbation and global goodwill alone are arguably reason enough for TOMS Shoes and Honest Tea to run programs like this, but there is also a more concrete return in the form of stability in their supply chains.

So besides altruism, we have two more compelling reasons for businesses to invest in host communities: One is to ensure the kind of stability that is conducive to doing business. The second reason is economic; Henry Ford, for example, is said to have paid high wages, not just to attract top-notch talent, but also so that his workers could afford to buy his cars. Once a community has been lifted out of poverty, it becomes a potential trading partner, and its people become potential customers.

Education

A community's general good health and relative prosperity is important, but the value of a *well-educated* workforce is incalculable. This is why Cargill goes to great lengths to provide education in the farming communities from which it sources agricultural products. CEO David MacLennan explained to me what the company does, where, and why.

"One of the four areas for us in sustainability is farmer education and farmer livelihood. In India I met a Sikh farmer from Punjab, which is up in the north of India. He's taken his dairy farm from roughly sixty cows to close to two hundred—about triple what he had before. I asked him how he did that, and he said it's because of Cargill: 'You taught me how to use nutrition in feeding my cows; you gave me feed formulations that made them healthier, which made them grow, which increased my production of milk.' He's reinvesting in his farm, and in his own quality of life, and his cycle of well-being has improved as a result.

"And so it's farmer education and then reinvesting in the communities where we're building our plants. It's directly related to ending poverty and hunger, but it's really through the instruction of sustainable farming methods. In Zambia we've trained about one hundred thousand farmers on sustainable farming techniques—when you plant, how you protect your crops from wind, when you water, how much water you use, how much fertilizer and herbicides you use. We went to a co-op and the farmer said that because of the training that we had done with him, he increased his yields by over 50 percent, which allowed him to reinvest in growing his farm. And to me, that's the virtuous cycle of being a global leader in nourishing people, [and] helping to end poverty and hunger. For example, in Vietnam, we've built over sixty schools.[35] There was a government official in Vietnam

---

35 MacLennan is perhaps being modest here. Cargill actually built its *seventieth* school in Vietnam in 2014: http://www.cargill.com/news/releases/2014/ NA31708653.jsp

who referred to us as the school company. And to me that's a measure of how we're known for something other than the products we produce. We're known for what we're doing in the community. And I think those are nonquantitative measures of success.

"Our goals in sustainability are around four areas: land use, water, climate change, and farmer livelihoods. And if they're certified to meet the Cargill Cocoa Promise, we pay them more money, and they, in turn, reinvest that in their community."

Cargill's Cocoa Promise is itself an admirable example of a company caring about the well-being of the communities where it does business. Much like coffee and sugar, cocoa is often obtained through murky supply chains in which abuses are rampant and farmers are not paid a fair price for the products of their labor. The Cargill Cocoa Promise is an attempt to rectify this situation as much as possible. It reads, in part, "Our aim is to accelerate progress towards a transparent global cocoa supply chain, enable farmers and their communities to achieve better incomes and living standards, and deliver a sustainable supply of cocoa and chocolate products."

The Dow Chemical Company has employees in every corner of the globe, and for this reason, the company takes the welfare of the communities in which those employees live seriously. This is why Dow Chemical's 2025 Sustainability Goals include assessing and working to improve quality of life in every country in which it does business.[36] Dow CEO Andrew Liveris told me about his experience with the company's Thailand operations.

"Dow has always exported its standards . . . when I was in Thailand as a general manager in the '80s, constructing Dow Chemical plants there, we looked at the highest government standards [for containing] waste, containing emissions, and ensuring worker safety. [These were]

36 Dow 2025 Sustainability Goals: http://www.dow.com/en-us/science-and-sustainability/sustainability-reporting/engaging-employees-for-impact

Department of Labor equivalent standards, and we compared them to the highest standards we were held to around the world. So we built our facilities, we trained our workers, we paid our workers, we helped our communities, and we upgraded facilities around us, and made it a wide net. In other words, we included all stakeholders, including government. And by so doing, you could argue we were uncompetitive on a cost-to-produce basis compared to our local competitors who didn't fulfill those standards; they just fulfilled their current government standards. But maybe five to ten years later, the Thai government adopted our standards.

"[Doing all this] sells more Dow technology, and it creates a value proposition that enables us to bring all stakeholders to a higher standard. And when that higher standard is obtained, humanity benefits, hunger starts to get eliminated. We are one of the few companies that have invested to that higher standard."

This has been the longest chapter of this book up to this point. Why? Because its message resonates with one of the book's overarching themes: give back to the communities where you do business, and they'll give back to you in the long run.

Key Takeaways

1. It is a moral imperative to take care not to poison the air or water in communities where you do any kind of business.

2. Your company bears some degree of ethical responsibility for the well-being and sustenance of communities that become economically dependent on you.

3. Taking care of the people who live and work in your company's orbit ensures the long-term sustainability of your supply chain.

4. Investing in education and other long-term prosperity initiatives improves the quality of the talent pool that may someday produce your best and brightest employees.

5. Once a community has been lifted out of poverty, it becomes a potential trading partner, and its people become potential customers.

CHAPTER 6

FORM GOOD PARTNERSHIPS

"Many ideas grow better when transplanted into another mind than in the one where they sprung up."

—**Oliver Wendell Holmes Sr.**, author, physician, and father of Supreme Court Justice Oliver Wendell Holmes Jr.

N ot long after you decide to embrace global sustainability as part of your business model, you are likely to have an epiphany: you're not alone. Many other business leaders feel, as you do, that a company can do well by doing good, and that success entails certain responsibilities. In the wake of this epiphany, the logical next course of action would be to seek out these like-minded individuals and give some thought to what you might be able to accomplish together.

By acting in concert and pooling their resources, two or more businesses can often achieve shared goals more effectively than any one company could on its own—often at a considerably lower cost.

Partnerships with local or national governments are also desirable. Government and business, acting together, can accomplish a great deal by utilizing each other's strengths and compensating for each other's weaknesses. The private sector is famously much more adept than government at getting things done efficiently and holding down costs; after all, an efficiently run company cannot be overburdened with bureaucracy. Government, on the other hand, has authority to act in ways that businesses cannot, and it has, for all practical purposes, an almost limitless budget with which to work.

Partnerships with NGOs—nongovernmental organizations—are probably the easiest types of alliances to form. NGOs are mission-driven, which means that the people who work for them are the best-informed people to be found in matters related to an NGO's particular area of concern. Whatever cause resonates most strongly with you, there is almost certainly an organization out there that has been devoted to it for years, or even decades. In fact, chances are that there are dozens of organizations dedicated to your pet cause, and that you already privately support at least one of them. Many NGOs subsist largely on donations, and therefore, readily welcome partnerships with deep-pocketed companies.

Businesses, governments, and NGOs can and often do work together for their mutual benefit and for the benefit of global society as a whole. Each has its virtues; each has its vices. In this chapter we will look at some examples of all three types of partnerships and learn what makes them work.

Collaboration vs. Competition

Collaboration, rather than vicious competition, is going to be the future model for sustainability. Consider the definition of *synergy*: 1+1 = 3.

That speaks to the importance of collaboration. No one individual or company has all the answers, and time and resources are finite. We each have the opportunity to ask, "How do I get the greatest amount of leverage from my time and available resources? How and where do we find inspiration for solutions?" I submit that we can evolve our thinking at a faster rate through collaboration; as the cliché goes, two heads are better than one.

Human beings have a natural propensity for competition; we are hardwired for it. But if we can find ways to collaborate with those who share our values on the topic of sustainability, we will find that many of our principles are transferable, regardless of the industry in which we work. You don't have to share trade secrets with your competitors (although some business leaders do, as we will learn shortly), but it isn't always necessary to mistrust them. If you don't feel comfortable meeting with and sharing with competitors, then find noncompeting company leaders with whom you can share your best practices and initiatives.[37]

DSM's Feike Sijbesma is one CEO who *is* willing to share some of his company's intellectual property with his collaborative partners.

"We started the collaboration between DSM—the world's largest player in nutritional ingredients—and the United Nations' World Food Programme because nutritional deficiencies are a big problem. And I said to them, 'You can use all my technologies in this area for free. You cannot resell it, because then we're out of business. But for the poorest people in the world, you can use it.'"

It is, of course, one thing to share a company's discoveries and inventions with the UN, and another thing entirely to share them with one's competitors. What CEO would do such a thing?

Kering's François-Henri Pinault does, and he told me why: "One key component of our way of practicing sustainability is that it has to

---

37   One way to do this would be through my Sustainability Peer Groups program; for details on this please visit www.SustainabilityPeerGroups.com

be open-source. If we just do that for competitive advantage, that's the wrong attitude for us. It can be a competitive disadvantage if we do nothing, certainly, but everything has to be shared. If this move is made in the private sector, we will have a better chance to change something."

Pinault isn't making an idle promise here. Kering has developed an innovative tool, the Environmental Profit & Loss Account (E P&L), which "makes the invisible impacts of business visible, quantifiable, and comparable."[38] The company's stated reason for this is that, "We can no longer see resources as infinite or ignore externalities. We needed a way to see the reality behind our supply chains, to understand our environmental impact so that we can reduce it." (We'll learn more about Kering's E P&L in chapter 9.)

Kering also shares with its competitors a leather-tanning method that most companies would consider a trade secret.

"One big process in our industry is the tanning of leather," Pinault says, "and for durability and quality reasons, we're using chrome tanning, which is heavily detrimental to the environment. So around three or four years ago, we asked ourselves, *Can we tan with the same type of quality and durability without heavy metals?* And I, myself, met some chemical companies, engineers, and scientists, who were unanimous in saying we don't have any techniques to tan with the level of quality we require, other than using chrome.

"They didn't say it's not *possible*; they said, 'we don't know.' So we decided to do some research and development to try to see if we could find an answer—even though this question had never been raised before. So we worked with a German university, and after two years, we found through Gucci a way of tanning leathers without any heavy metals. Of course, it's 25 percent more expensive, but one reason is that the process cannot tan a certain quality of skin—so the skins that you're not using in that new process are considered to be waste. This is the main

---

38 Kering website: http://www.kering.com/en/sustainability/epl

source of price difference. So now we're working on finding a channel of distribution through which we could resell those skins that we're not using anymore in that process, in order to lower the price difference.

"If you ask yourself questions at the very early stages of your processes, you may find surprising solutions. In the case of leather tanning, besides the extra cost due to the fact that you're not using older skins, in terms of water consumption and energy consumption, it's 20 to 30 percent cheaper than the regular way of tanning leather. So, if we can reduce the price difference by reselling those skins, the new process will be much cleaner *and* cheaper at the end of the day than the previous process.

"So everything that we do [regarding sustainability]—the E P&L, for example—has been shared with the community. I don't keep anything for myself; the techniques that we have found for leather tanning are shared on a free basis with our competitors. It's better to try to reach the community and to move together; this is why I joined The B Team when Richard Branson asked me to. But we have to be all together, pushing in the same direction."

The B Team Pinault refers to is a global nonprofit initiative co-founded by Richard Branson in order to bring together CEOs and business leaders from all over the world. Its objective is to encourage businesses everywhere to adopt sustainable practices to ensure our collective future:

> Founded in the belief that the private sector can and must redefine both its responsibilities and its own terms of success, we are developing a 'Plan B' for concerted, positive action that will ensure business becomes a driving force for social, environmental, and economic benefit. Plan A—where business has been motivated primarily by profit—is no longer an option. Business is now waking up to the reality that if we carry on

using the natural resources of the world unsustainably, they'll quite simply run out.

If we leverage the many positives of business—the spirit of enterprise, innovation, and entrepreneurship that has helped realise improvements in quality of life and enabled technological and scientific progress—we can create an unprecedented era of sustainable, inclusive prosperity for all. The time has come for us to play our part in finding the solutions. That's why we formed The B Team.[39]

Sounds familiar, doesn't it? The B Team's goals are exactly what I'm advocating in this book! Perhaps not coincidentally, quite a few of the people profiled in these pages are The B Team members. Besides Richard Branson and François-Henri Pinault, this list also includes Marc Benioff, Guilherme Leal, Blake Mycoskie, Ratan Tata, and Paul Polman.

Polman in particular is something of an omnipresent superhero for the global-sustainability movement (an impression you may already have gotten from previous chapters). Under his leadership, Unilever began working with Ben & Jerry's to replace the ice cream freezer cases we see in supermarkets and convenience stores with newer cases that rely on environmentally friendly technology rather than hydrofluorocarbons (HFCs). In 2011 alone, according to Unilever's website, the company rolled out twenty-two thousand of these new freezers in non-US markets, resulting in a reduction of twelve thousand tons of CO_2 emissions. And the eventual goal is to eliminate HFC freezers altogether.

"What we are trying to do here is put the right groups of people together," Polman says. "And by doing that you can create that tipping point on anything. We brought together companies like Coke, Pepsi, and Nestlé—normally competitors—to change the cooler cabinets for

---

39 The B-Team website: http://bteam.org/about/

ice cream or beverages to natural refrigerants. That's 3 percent of global warming. But it takes effort to put these coalitions together."

Unilever seems to be very much in the habit of collaborating with other companies to achieve universally desirable ends: the company has also begun working on a "Sustainability Platform" in conjunction with PepsiCo, The Coca-Cola Company, Save the Children, and a number of market-research companies. The ambitiously stated purpose of this initiative, called Paragon, is "to tackle the seventeen-point plan of the UN Global Goals—end poverty, combat climate change, and fight injustice and inequality around the world."[40]

The idea, according to Paragon's website, is this:

A steering committee made up of clients, research agencies, academics, NGOs, and government partners will convene on a quarterly basis to agree on three key questions aligned to the UN Global Goals. These questions will be added to any research conducted by the agencies for their clients during that quarter. This will enable the generation of granular data and insights on issues affecting people around the world. The data will be hosted on a single platform to democratise the information and facilitate a simple and user-friendly access. The data will be accessible to anyone and everyone who is signed up to the Paragon initiative, allowing them to formulate fact-based programmes for creating a brighter future.

Another of Unilever's collaborations with its corporate peers involves The Dow Chemical Company (about whom we will hear quite a bit more before the end of this chapter). Dow collaborated with Unilever to develop POLYOX™ polymers for Unilever's Lifebuoy soap, which costs ten cents a bar and lasts an entire month, helping to support

---

40   Paragon: http://www.paragonpartnerships.com/

Unilever's Sustainable Living Plan.[41] And adding to this complex web of synergy, both companies are members of the World Business Council for Sustainable Development (WBCSD), "a CEO-led organization of forward-thinking companies that galvanizes the global business community to create a sustainable future for business, society, and the environment."[42]

The WBCSD was founded at the time of the 1992 Rio de Janeiro Earth Summit. Its purpose was to ensure that business interests had a voice at the forum. It was the brainchild of Stephan Schmidheiny, a Swiss entrepreneur who believed that business had an obligation to contribute to sustainable development, and that it would benefit the bottom line to do so. Like The B Team I mentioned earlier, WBSCD's members include many of the companies whose leaders are featured in this book: The Dow Chemical Company, DSM, Kering, KPMG, Natura, Salesforce, Unilever, and the Tata group.

Partnerships with NGOs

As I noted earlier, NGOs tend to be enthusiastic recipients of corporate support—provided such support does not compromise their missions— and their expertise with global-sustainability issues makes them excellent working partners.

Unilever

"[Without assistance], it would be impossible for us to reach a billion children with handwashing programs," Unilever's Paul Polman told me. "We would be bankrupt if we tried to do that. But by working with all these NGOs, we have already reached nearly 350 million in the last four years, which is more than any government could do."

---

41   Dow website: http://www.dow.com/news/press-releases/dow%20and%20
      unilever%20help%20deliver%20a%20healthier%20world%20one%20touch%20
      at%20a%20time%20for%20global%20handwashing%20day
42   WBCSD website: http://www.wbcsd.org/about.aspx

Unilever's most ambitious and potentially far-reaching sustainability initiative is also its simplest, in a way: handwashing. The simple act of washing one's hands with soap for twenty seconds does more than just about anything else to curb the spread of disease. Through its Lifebuoy soap brand—and in partnership with various governments, The World Bank Group, and a host of NGOs, including Save the Children, Oxfam, and UNICEF—Unilever is conducting a public-health-education campaign designed to prevent the 1.1 million preventable diarrhea-related child deaths that occur across the developing world each year.[43] Unilever works with schools to encourage children to wash their hands at mealtimes and other critical points during the day, and has assisted with the retrofitting of water pumps in many places to make sanitation more broadly accessible.[44]

Unilever is also involved with partnerships meant ultimately to address world hunger via sustainable agriculture.

"We are rapidly depleting our land services and our soil," Polman says. "We could feed two hundred million more people by only using 12 percent of degraded land. So instead of cutting more forests, you have to make the world understand that it is better to invest in degraded lands and in sustainable agriculture, bringing the yield per acre up, getting out of the heavy pesticide use, better water management, etc. So again, there are big alliances that we have created—the New Vision for Agriculture, Grow Africa, Climate-Smart Agriculture—and these are all alliances meant to get more people involved in sustainable agriculture."

---

43 Lifebuoy website: http://www.lifebuoy.com/socialmission/
44 Leon Kaye, "Unilever's Handwashing Campaign Goes Beyond CSR and Saves Lives," *Triple Pundit*, April 22, 2015: http://www.triplepundit.com/special/disrupting-short-termism/unilevers-handwashing-campaign-goes-beyond-csr-and-saves-lives/

Save the Children

While researching this book and looking for connections between NGOs and business, I found that the names of certain groups kept recurring in the material I read. Save the Children stands out in particular. This ninety-seven-year-old organization is involved in one way or another with many of the companies whose CEOs I interviewed for this project. They are participants in Unilever's handwashing campaign, and they are partnered in one way or another with Carnival Australia, This Bar Saves Lives, and TOMS Shoes, among others.

TOMS Shoes founder Blake Mycoskie says, "Big organizations like Partners In Health and Save the Children help distribute millions of shoes for us, as do small ones like Coprodeli, a community-development organization based in Peru. So, yeah, we use nonprofits and NGOs on the ground that already are really entrenched in the community and know what the communities' needs are, which enables them to distribute the shoes in the proper way."

DSM and the World Food Programme

As I noted in a previous chapter, DSM's Feike Sijbesma is a man of extraordinary humanitarian accomplishments, and has been duly recognized as such; he has been honored with the UN's Humanitarian of the Year Award and its Leaders of Change Award. Under Sijbesma's leadership, DSM has collaborated with the World Food Programme on initiatives designed to reduce food insecurity throughout the developing world and encourage farmers to adopt sustainable farming methods in order to prevent farmland from becoming degraded and useless.[45]

---

45   WFP website: https://www.wfp.org/For%20Companies/blog/dsm-ceo-feike-sijbesma-visits-wfp-projects-ethiopia

Richard Branson, Virgin, and The Elders

Many of the partnerships and initiatives discussed in this chapter and throughout this book are aimed at addressing problems related to poverty—specifically hunger, malnutrition, and lack of access to medical care. However, there is another global problem that is often the underlying cause of these ills and others: armed conflict. When I spoke to Richard Branson, he told me about his work with an organization called The Elders, which was formed by Nelson Mandela in 2007 in order to deal with this problem. Mandela died in 2013, but The Elders are still operating, and the group is currently chaired by former UN Secretary-General Kofi Annan.

"So, at Virgin, we have a foundation," Branson told me. "We've set up a number of organizations to try to drive some of the big issues of the world, so we set up The Elders with Nelson Mandela and Graça Machel and Archbishop Tutu to concentrate on conflict issues to try to use their moral authority to go into conflict areas and knock heads together, either behind the scenes or in front of the scenes, to try to bring about peace in difficult situations."

Why should any for-profit enterprise care about this kind of work? Because war and civil unrest are bad for business, bad for nations' economies, and bad for people trying to make a living.

"If you have conflict, everything else falls apart," Branson says, "as we've seen in Syria. And if you have conflict, you can't worry about education, you can't worry about health, and you can't worry about all the conventional things that a country needs to worry about. It's just survival."

The Dow Chemical Company

The Dow Chemical Company has more partners than a pretty girl at a square dance. What follows is just a partial listing of the company's many sustainability-related partnerships with NGOs and governments:

- Dow is one of the founders of AgroLAC 2025—a collaboration with The Nature Conservancy—whose purpose is to reduce food waste and improve farmland production. This collaboration builds on Dow's Sustainable Livestock Initiative, which has increased production on degraded pasture land in Brazil by a factor of four and is expected to help conserve the Amazon rainforest.

- Dow partnered with AgriStewards, a mission group started by farmers in Lebanon, Indiana, to provide agricultural training to farmers in Kenya in order to improve their farming practices.

- Dow is the largest shareholder in WaterHealth International, a company focused on providing clean water to communities in the developing world. More than five hundred WaterHealth Centers are deployed in India and Africa. WHI's goal is to serve one hundred million people by 2020. WHI sells water in India for one-tenth the price of equivalent quality water from other sources . . . and in Africa, the price is fifteen- to twenty-times lower.

- In the 1980s, Dow became the first national corporate partner of Habitat for Humanity®. Since then, Dow has contributed more than $70 million to the organization and helped build or repair more than forty-five thousand homes in twenty-nine countries. Last year, Dow and Habitat for Humanity® expanded their partnership to address global housing and sanitation issues in Ethiopia, Argentina, Colombia, and Nepal.

Partnerships with Governments

As I said earlier, governments have power that private enterprises, such as NGOs and businesses, do not have. The authority and financial resources that governments have at their command, combined with the operational efficiency of most for-profit businesses, can achieve impressive results.

One excellent example of this kind of synergy at work is Dow's collaboration with local and national governments in China and the Netherlands to improve water treatment and purification. In the Dutch city of Terneuzen, Dow helped authorities devise a way to reuse city water up to three times, resulting in energy-savings equivalent to the CO_2 emissions of thirteen thousand cars every year. In China, the company's Safe Water for Kids program partnered with the China Women's Development Foundation to donate water-purification systems to four rural schools in western China's Shaanxi Province, thereby improving drinking-water safety for approximately two thousand school children.

Natura's Guilherme Leal has been involved with government in an even more direct way: in 2010, he actually ran for the position of vice president in his native Brazil, alongside Green Party candidate Marina Silva. The ticket finished in third place, and Leal decided not to run for office again after that.

"After some reflection, I became aware that it's not my personal vocation to be in the front line of politics," he told me. "But I still am convinced that without politics, we cannot promote the change we want. So I decided after my experience in 2010 to find the new generation of politicians [who will run] in the future and bring them together across the party lines to promote sustainability, to promote ethics in politics, and to help them share their experiences, in the expectation that in some years, we could have an important group of politicians embedded on those values and practices."

To this end, Leal has put together a group called RAPS, a Portuguese acronym for *Rede* (network) *Ação* (action) *Política* (Politics) *Sustentabilidade* (sustainability). The group's mission, according to an English translation of its website, is to "Contribute to the improvement of the political process and the quality of Brazilian democracy through the training of political leaders committed to the values and principles of ethics, transparency, and sustainability."

Unilever works with governments around the world to train small farmers in modern agricultural and business methods.

"I was just with Prime Minister Modi in India," Paul Polman told me. "He's asking me to [involve] Hindustan Unilever [in this project] because he sees us doing it. That's our business model. We've said we want to reach five million more people in our value chain to improve their livelihoods, including small-holder farmers, and we've just signed an agreement that will enable us to reach a million more [of them]. Now, we could never do this alone; we don't have the capabilities to reach that many farmers, aggregate them, and train them in management, agricultural techniques, board management, social standards, etc.

"So you work with these different organizations, and as you do this, you secure your value chain, you provide the livelihoods that undoubtedly will come back to you, because obviously, we cannot prosper if these communities don't prosper, and our business model will become stronger [because of these programs]. And that's a business model that's not run by quarters; that's a business model that's run by years."[46]

Under ideal circumstances, all three types of entities—businesses, governments, and NGOs—can come together to maximize the power of all three to address the problems of poverty, health, gender inequality, and disease. The Millennium Villages Project aims to do just that in ten of the poorest countries in Africa by improving access to clean water, education, basic health care, sanitation, and improved agricultural techniques. The ultimate goal of the Millennium Villages project is to provide communities living in extreme poverty with an opportunity to lift themselves out of it.

---

46   "A business model that's run by years." Remember what we learned in chapter 2 about long-term thinking?

The Millennium Villages Project was initially funded by private contributions—including $50 million from George Soros—and has expanded as local African governments have gotten involved. In addition to the governments of the African countries where the project is being conducted, support has also come from the governments of Finland, Ireland, Japan, and Norway. The project was spearheaded by the Earth Institute at Columbia University, and it is now involved in partnerships with several UN organizations, including UNAIDS, UNDP, UNFPA, UNICEF, UNOPS, and the World Food Programme. Its corporate partners include KPMG (which has contributed $1.5 million[47]) and Unilever, among many others.

The Millennium Villages Project also has guiding principles (see chapter 1 of this book for a reminder of the importance of these), which are summed up in its Millennium Promise:[48]

- Promote sustainable, scalable, community-led progress toward the achievement of the Millennium Development Goals through the use of scientifically validated interventions—one village at a time
- Ensure African ownership of the Millennium Development Goals, and work in partnership with African governments and regional groups
- Increase capacity and community empowerment in Africa through training and knowledge sharing with local African governments, NGOs, and village communities
- Partner with the public and private sectors, innovative NGOs, universities and leading experts, and the international donor

---

47 Business & Human Rights Resource Centre website: http://business-humanrights.org/en/kpmg-joins-the-millennium-villages-project-to-help-address-extreme-poverty-in-africa-tanzania

48 Millennium Villages Project website: http://millenniumvillages.org/millenniumpromise/?docID=861

community throughout Africa and the world to continually improve and coordinate development strategies

- Transform rural sub-subsistence farming economies into small-scale enterprise development economies and promote diversified entrepreneurs

The results that have been achieved by the combined efforts of these myriad companies, governments, and NGOs are impressive. In Pemba, Tanzania, for example, only 66 percent of children were enrolled in school before the start of the project. Dropout rates were high among those children who did attend school, and hunger exacerbated the problem of education; many children were unable to concentrate on their studies due to the effects of poor nutrition. Many of the locals earned their living by farming or fishing, but fish stocks were dwindling and the soil was degraded and unproductive.

Through the Millennium Villages Project, KPMG and its partners built numerous schoolhouses and taught locals to harvest seaweed profitably. Pemba was also connected to the electricity grid, and access to vaccinations and basic health care were expanded, reducing death from preventable illnesses.[49]

Key Takeaways

1. By acting in concert and pooling their resources, two or more businesses can often achieve shared goals more effectively than any one company could on its own.
2. Much can be achieved by combining the authority and resources of government with the efficiency of for-profit business.
3. Much can be achieved by combining the expertise and passion of NGOs with the financial resources of for-profit business.

---

49 KPMG YouTube Channel: https://www.youtube.com/watch?v=KjowOftJMjM

4. Much of the world's poverty and political inequality arises from armed conflict, and businesses should care about this, not just because such concern is humane, but also because conflict is bad for commerce.

5. Businesses can often benefit by eschewing viciously competitive strategies in favor of mutually beneficial collaboration.

$\boxed{\;\rightarrow \text{CHAPTER 7} \leftarrow\;}$

FIND WAYS TO REDUCE WASTE

"Use it up, wear it out, make it do, or do without!"
—Old Proverb

To waste any kind of resource—food, energy, land, time, or money—is disgraceful. Everyone on Earth understands this at some basic level. As children, many of us were shamed into finishing our supper (even the broccoli!) by our mothers' reproachful reminders that hungry children in Africa would gratefully wolf down our leftover food if they could . . . the implication being that we had no right to throw it away. Human beings abhor waste almost instinctively—perhaps we are hardwired that way—and most of us understand it to be a kind of sin that transcends religion.

And yet waste is ubiquitous. We live on a planet with limited resources, and our growing population is consuming those resources at an alarming rate. It is incumbent upon everyone to find ways to reduce waste in order to ensure our global sustainability.

Attacking Waste within Your Company

Waste is the invisible enemy of profit, and even the tiniest leak will eventually empty a bucket. Waste of natural resources hurts not only the environment, but also a company's bottom line. The Dow Chemical Company understands this, which is why the company boasts of having saved more than $6 billion from investments in sustainability since 1995.[50]

The simplest way to reduce waste in your own company is to look at material and energy inefficiencies in your offices and in your office procedures. Some businesses find they are able to achieve energy savings via cloud computing. Salesforce embraces this solution.

"We help our customers save carbon and energy," says the company's chief philanthropy officer, Suzanne DiBianca. "When organizations move business applications to the cloud, they reduce energy use and their carbon footprints by as much as 98 percent compared to on-premises solutions."

Guidance founder Jon Provisor says, "We have hundreds of servers at our facility. We [looked] at all our servers and replaced them with low-energy-usage servers. If you look at the single biggest draw of power in our organization, it is all the desktop machines and the servers in the co-location facilities versus travel or any other expenditure."

Guidance also encourages employees to eschew printing in favor of sharing files electronically.

---

50 Sustainable Brands website: http://www.sustainablebrands.com/news_and_views/brand_innovation/neil_hawkins/redefining_role_business_achieve_un_sustainable_develop

"Everything that we can control, we reduce, we reuse, we recycle—the three R's, right? You will see blue bins next to every [desk in our offices]. We challenged the company to go paperless as much as possible, digitize every presentation for customers, and send PDFs versus printouts. And not only do we have recycling for company products, but also anyone can bring in old monitors, computers, or other e-waste products, and we have a recycling service that picks them up and disposes of them properly. I once had some speakers from the Sierra Club come in, and they said that they don't even do these simple things like have recycle bins near every trash receptacle or encourage people to go digital versus printing. Our committee literally tries to think about every possible way that we could optimize that solution."

Energy Waste

Reducing energy waste is one of the most effective ways for a company to simultaneously save money and reduce its carbon footprint. Whole Foods co-CEO Walter Robb told me how his company is attacking energy waste in its stores and elsewhere in its operations:

"Our view is that every kilowatt-hour of energy saved is basically a pound less carbon in the atmosphere. And so our goal is to reduce our energy use by 20 percent per square foot by 2020 . . . and we're at about 14 percent now. Our new stores are incredibly efficient. We also have a large number of solar stores, and we're increasing the number of those.

"We're also working on an initiative to reduce water use in the same quantities by 20 to 25 percent, but our main focus has been to reduce our energy use through investment in remodels and upgrades in the store systems, and in adding doors into the freezers and the coolers. All those steps are being taken to just keep pounding down the energy use, because the least expensive energy is the energy that you don't use.

"We have lots of other initiatives with respect to composting our waste produce: we box it up, send it back, and compost it. We were the first grocer to do the 100 percent recycled paper bag. We eliminated plastic bags.

"But I guess I would highlight the energy use as probably being the most significant overall in terms of impact. We have biofuel trucks that we're messing around with, using recycled cooking oil. And, of course, we also have done a lot of things on our packaging . . . we've eliminated the polystyrene. We have worked with our suppliers to incrementally improve packaging standards for products. So all those efforts are under this broader rubric of sustainability.

"Ultimately you've got to look more widely at how you're landing in the world: what's your responsibility in the world as a company and how can you contribute to the world in a way that makes business sense? The two are not disjoined; they're connected, and to be successful, you're going to have to do that."

For most companies, curbing energy waste means finding ways to use electricity more efficiently in stores, offices, factories, and warehouses. If you have a fleet of trucks, however (as Whole Foods does), then fuel inefficiency is an additional energy consideration. And if you have a fleet of 747s (as Richard Branson's Virgin Atlantic does), that consideration becomes much more important.

"Our spaceship company is working on trying to come up with clean fuels for airplanes," Branson says, "and obviously, planes are becoming more fuel efficient because of carbon fiber rather than metal, and that's great. But it would be absolutely wonderful if we could actually power our planes on fuel that is carbon-neutral. We now have a 747, for instance, at Virgin Galactic, and we've got a guy whose job is to try to make sure that 747 is run on clean fuels as much as possible— and, if possible, clean fuels that are not eating into the food supply, so maybe algae-based fuels or Isobutanol-based fuels. A number of other airlines have gotten together to work on this as well, but we've got seven hundred technicians at Virgin Galactic—so let's let them use their brainpower to try to sort this problem out. "

Unilever and Dow on Food Waste and Sustainable Agriculture

When I spoke to Paul Polman, he had a lot to say about food waste, land waste, and sustainable agriculture:

"If you want to cut costs in a company and you say you're introducing another cost-cutting program, people will yawn and say, 'I've heard that before: new boss, new savings program.' But if you say, 'We are going to cut food waste in our system because there are still eight hundred million people going to bed hungry and we are going to take responsibility for ensuring that these people don't go bed hungry anymore,' then attacking the waste in your value chain takes on a whole other dimension.

"So, 30 to 40 percent of the food that gets produced in this world gets wasted. If food waste were a country, it would be the third biggest climate emitter after China and the US. So we have created industry coalitions with [organizations such as] WRI [the World Resources Institute]. We also work with governments, and we create alliances to take the food waste out of the system because you cannot do all of that alone. It is good for the climate, without any doubt. It is good for our planet in terms of land use and deforestation. But it is also good from a moral point of view to ensure that people who go to bed hungry at least have a chance to get the minimum that you would expect for people— an opportunity to feed themselves.

"But we go way beyond that; we are conscious of the materials we use. So all of our factories are now zero waste to landfill, [and we are] the first company, I believe, of our size or magnitude that has achieved that. It saves us €75 million on landfill costs, and it just makes common sense.

"We are rapidly depleting our land services and our soil. We could feed two hundred million more people by only using 12 percent of degraded land. So instead of cutting more forests, you have to make the world understand that it is better to invest in degraded lands and in sustainable agriculture, bringing the yield per acre up."

The point here is that reduction in wasted land will make agribusiness more profitable, in addition to reducing certain long-term threats to the environment *and* addressing the injustice of hunger among nearly one seventh of the world's population.

Polman isn't alone in taking an interest in agricultural sustainability. Andrew Liveris told me about Dow Chemical's involvement in a project aimed at reclaiming degraded farmland.

"We're one of the founders of an institution called AgroLAC 2025. It's a collaboration with the Inter-American Development Bank and The Nature Conservancy. We're applying technology to reduce food waste by improving production from current lands, and we have this technology that actually stops pastureland being degraded by grazing cattle. And we're putting that technology in place through AgroLAC, which is a consorter approach using multiple stakeholders—everyone in the so-called food chain. We've already implemented this on a million hectares of degraded pastureland and raised the production on that land by an average of four times . . . and in some areas, by as much as eight times.

"The most critical outcome is that, not only does it get more food into the food chain in countries in Latin America and South America, but it also stops the need to cut down the Amazon rainforest. So it has an impact on the climate-change goal.

"And this is a way of approaching a solution in collaboration. Yes, it sells more Dow technology, but it creates a value proposition that enables us to bring all stakeholders to a higher standard. And when that higher standard is obtained, humanity benefits, and hunger starts to get eliminated."

"A Circular Economy"—Saving Money
by Reducing Packaging Waste

The Dow Chemical Company's above-described work to address the problem of farmland degradation—i.e., wasteful land use—is commendable, and it's aligned with Dow's stated 2025 Sustainability Goals, which include a commitment to a "circular economy" in which products that would once have been considered waste, are recycled.[51]

Pacific Seafood's Greenshield® boxes are another good example of this kind of commitment. Despite its dependence on a healthy natural environment, the seafood industry has a history of using environmentally unfriendly packaging, including polystyrene foam containers and heavily waxed (and therefore, unrecyclable) boxes. To address this problem, Pacific Seafood partnered with the Georgia-Pacific manufacturing company to produce the 100 percent recyclable Greenshield® boxes.

"They're 100 percent biodegradable," Pacific Seafood CEO Frank Dulcich told me, "and they can be used for composting, etc. That was us and Georgia-Pacific, working together." (Another example of the kind of collaboration we discussed in chapter 6!)

The Greenshield® boxes are not Pacific's only packaging innovation aimed at reducing waste. Dulcich told me about an even more exciting development: shelf-life extension packaging.

"These animals we harvest can live anywhere from three years all the way up to thirty years. And here is the business problem: Retailers sell fresh fish out of what's called *the self-service case,* which is where you would go and buy the tray-wrapped seafood. The retailers wrap the fish, and then in three days, they throw the product away. Once the product is thrown away, it is called *shrink.* If the retailer has a 20 percent shrink in fresh seafood, that means they're throwing 20 percent of their seafood away. Because of this, two things happen: One, the

---

51 Dow website: http://www.dow.com/en-us/science-and-sustainability/sustainability-reporting/advancing-circular-economy

cost of seafood for consumers must be increased by 20 percent to equalize the loss to the retailer. And two, you're discarding great food that somebody could have eaten.

"We have developed a process called 'shelf-life extension,' a packaging technology that enables us to create for the retailer a shelf life of not three days, but twenty-one days. And we will actually be guaranteeing our customers fourteen days to sell the product. With this new technology, we're able to give the retailer a 500 percent additional selling time and provide an eating experience to the consumer that is equal to the first day the product was processed.

"In all the tests and trials we've completed to date, if we harvest and process the product within our vertical-integrated cold chain, every product tested achieved a minimum of twenty-one days of shelf life, [throughout which time] you and I could sit with our families at a meal and eat the product together and have a great experience."

Package Lightweighting

Pacific Seafood's Greenshield® boxes are an example of a growing practice known as *package lightweighting*, which means exactly what the term suggests. Honest Tea's Seth Goldman recommends this practice, not just because it benefits the environment by cutting down on the amount of plastic used, but also because it's cheaper.

"We'll certainly look for packaging savings. My point of view on the packaging in general is that its value is neutral. And if I can lightweight my packaging, that's a good step for our business financially, as well as environmentally. So I'm happy to look for the cheapest sustainable option I can find."

TerraCycle's Tom Szaky agrees, although he finds the subject to be a bit more complex.

"So the idea of the circular economy when it comes to consumer goods is, how do you make the packaging easier to recover and put right back into the same product? That is a simplified example, but every major consumer-product company in the world is lightweighting their packaging. They are using fewer resources to make the package, which has a very good short-term sustainability story to it, without question. There is less resource use. However, when you move away from a glass jar to package your pasta sauce in a sachet, you have used fewer resources, but you have also made it significantly less recyclable. So this is the challenge. There is huge discussion about sustainability and its derivatives, and about what constitutes a circular economy, and so on. But what actually happens, in many cases, is not what is being discussed. That is the part that is the overall challenge.

"So it is a journey. We need to keep showing as many strong case studies as we can, but there are huge forces out there, as well, that we have to contend with."

Profiting by Minimizing the Waste of Natural Resources

Reducing waste also means maximizing the return you get from resources you take from the natural world. Frank Dulcich makes sure his company never misses an opportunity to do this, as he told me during our interview.

"In 1995 we had been in production for ten years and we were starting to get involved in the fishing side. We began to do research on how to maximize the return on each marine species we were harvesting. [For example], the processing industry in 1995 had a 19 percent recovery from a hundred pounds of shrimp. By continually monitoring and improving our work processes, our cook techniques, and our harvest techniques, we now are able to achieve double the protein return from the same animal. We've been able to reduce the fishing impact on shrimp by 50 percent and still return the same pounds to the consumer for consumption.

"We achieve this by understanding the biology and protein makeup of the entire animal. We maximize the value of all the parts—the organs, the protein, the shell—and look at them. We determine, in a perfect environment, how much real protein is in the animal, and then we work on processes to maximize the protein recovery.

"Our objective is to minimize impact on the marine environment and extract the maximum protein out of the product. With shrimp, for example, the industry was overcooking the product. Most of the protein was going down into the waste streams and not into the finished product. We have developed systems . . . to ensure that we extract the maximum protein."

Dulcich feels that this attention to waste prevention is a practice that enables Pacific Seafood Group to maintain its dominant leadership position in its industry, and that this careful husbandry of marine resources (again, recall the long-term thinking discussed in chapter 2) is necessary for the future of his industry.

To reiterate Pacific Seafood Group's principles from before: "By maximizing the recovery of our marine resources, we actually bring to market 20 percent more than our competitors. Because of our techniques, we're able to provide better return for the company, better pay for our people, and more food with less environmental impact. We can harvest fewer fish and feed more people because we understand the biology."

Waste Reduction as a Business Opportunity

Waste reduction would clearly be a valuable practice if its only benefit were short-term financial savings. In many instances, however, waste reduction can actually present business opportunities.

"We look at the waste streams," Dulcich told me, "and we found that on the shrimp shells, for example, there is value that we can [extract from] the shell . . . a blood clotter that helps for bandages. We haven't gotten into the pharmaceutical side of it yet, but we're looking at other ways to maximize the value of that.

"We also jointly developed Greenshield® boxes with Georgia-Pacific to look for a way to eliminate these wax boxes that were filling the landfills of the country," Dulcich told me. "One of our facilities was taking a hundred truckloads of polystyrene boxes a year to the dump; today, they take none. We are able to melt the polystyrene and export the final product to South Korea for molded frames and other uses."

Other business opportunities related to waste reduction abound. Recology asked some of its bigger restaurant customers to separate their food waste for composting, and offered them a reduced rate for their trouble. They now take seven hundred tons of organic matter per day from the city of San Francisco. Their giant competitor, Waste Management, may eventually lose business because they focus on maximizing profit by landfilling rather than recycling or composting, as many communities are beginning to prefer. This situation provides *opportunity* for companies like Recology—a subject we will discuss at greater length in the next chapter.

Key Takeaways

1. Waste is disgraceful, and deep down, everyone instinctively knows this.
2. Undetected waste eats away at profits.
3. Huge amounts of money can be saved by paying attention to energy waste, e.g., electricity, fuel, etc.
4. Money can be saved by working electronically whenever possible, rather than by printing documents.
5. Less wasteful packaging is cheaper.

CHAPTER 8

BE ADAPTABLE—AND SEIZE OPPORTUNITIES

"Some people will look at the UN Global Goals and think, OK, these are all the problems that charity has to solve. *I look at the Global Goals and think,* These are all entrepreneurial opportunities for new products.*"*

—**Blake Mycoskie**, founder, TOMS Shoes

"The good news is that sustainability is both a responsibility and a business opportunity. It's not just good for the planet, but clever for the business, and Natura is a good example of this."

—**Guilherme Leal**, co-chairman, Natura

Anyone who hopes to survive in business must understand the importance of adaptability. When conditions change in your environment—for example, if public demand for your product or service changes, or can be expected to change—you can't just bury your head in the sand and pretend it isn't happening. Consider what happened to Blockbuster Video when they failed to anticipate how the public would respond to Netflix. By the time Blockbuster recognized the danger they were in and made a few clumsy attempts to adapt to the public's desire for an easier way to rent movies, it was too late.

Or imagine what might have happened if the taxicab industry had had the foresight in 2009 to design phone apps that could enable users to summon cabs. They eventually did this, but by then it was too late to protect their monopoly . . . and it may yet turn out to be too late for their industry.

"I'm a biologist by training," says Feike Sijbesma of DSM, "and I quote Darwin a lot. Species survived by adapting themselves. The fittest were not the strongest or the biggest or the fastest species, but those that were the most *adaptable* [emphasis mine]. And I think that will be also true for countries and for organizations. We need to adapt to changing times, and if we don't adapt, we will run into big problems. And those who can make a change—an adaptation—will deal with these changes. This is an important part of my philosophy."

Big Changes in the World— and the Opportunities They Present

One important aspect of adaptability is the ability to anticipate big changes, and to be able to position oneself to take advantage of the *opportunities* those changes bring about. In this, too, Sijbesma sees an analogue to the journey our ancestors made out of the caves and trees.

"We are living a hundred and fifty years after the start of the Industrial Revolution," he reminded me. "And the Industrial Revolution brought prosperity for all of us, but it also created problems. A hundred and fifty years ago, we had fewer than a billion people living on the planet. Now we have over seven billion, and we are still growing. We should realize that we cannot continue on this path without [making] a fundamental change to how we live. We are depleting our resources and creating problems of inequality. We need to change the way we manage our natural resources, to move from the Fossil-Fuel Age into the Bio-renewable Age. And we need to make that transition to ensure prosperity for our children and for the next generation. At a certain moment, we will have moved into another age. And at that moment, we will look back at this age as only a blip in history.

"I use, sometimes, a comparison with moving out of the Stone Age. Some people argue that we still have enough coal for five hundred years, and oil and gas for maybe two hundred years, etc. And I say, true, but we didn't move out of the Stone Age because we ran out of stones. No, we moved out the Stone Age because there were better alternatives. And we will move out this Fossil-Fuel Age because there are better alternatives."

Paul Polman likewise sees big changes in our future: urbanization, he told me, is going to present our society with daunting challenges—and still more chances for alert businesspeople to make money.

"There are seven billion people in the world currently, and 50 percent of them—3.5 billion people—live in cities. The world [will soon be home] to 9 to 10 billion people, [and by that time] 70 percent will live in cities; that means 7 billion people. So we have to build as many new cities as we currently have on Earth. We have to build every two months another New York. So the question is, how do we spend the money? Are we making the buildings more energy efficient? Are we looking at smart transportation? So the money we are going to spend in the next sixty years is an enormous opportunity. It is $90 trillion [that will be spent] on urbanization. So this is an area of enormous opportunity, not a problem for businesses."

The Plight of the Poor—an Opportunity to Be Acted Upon

Polman continued in this vein, moving from the topic of urbanization to that of the underprivileged.

"The eight hundred million people who go to bed hungry is an enormous business opportunity. The 60 to 70 percent of people who don't wash their hands[52] is an enormous business opportunity."

This idea may seem counterintuitive to anyone who has grown accustomed to thinking of the poor as utterly powerless and lacking in agency, like baby birds that have fallen from the nest. But while the lives of the poor are hard, they are not helpless, and they have needs; indeed, their very condition, poverty, is defined by the needs of the people who live under its shadow. And as any astute businessman knows, where there is a need to be filled, there is money to be made.

The Tata group understands this principle, just as they understand their moral obligation to be a good corporate citizen in their native India, a country afflicted with some of the worst poverty in the developed world.

"The Tata group has always envisioned those at the bottom of the economic pyramid as producers and consumers of products, rather than as beneficiaries of charity," says a statement sent to me by a company spokesperson. "Therefore, it has continued to support creative, low-cost solutions to massive societal problems. There are an estimated 4.5 billion people in the world at 'the bottom of the pyramid' who live on $5 per day or less, and represent a $15 trillion economy that is poised to expand as these people join global markets as consumers and producers.

"The group launched Tata Swach water purifiers in the Indian market in 2009, with a vision of reducing the impact of waterborne diseases by providing safe drinking water to the masses. Using advanced silver nanotechnology, Tata Swach became one of the most affordable, point-

---

52 A reference to Unilever's handwashing campaign, described in chapter 6.

of-use water-purification solutions and continues to expand its presence in Indian households. The nonelectric Tata Swach water purifier [is designed to meet] the needs of rural consumers—many without access to electricity—and to meet the regulatory guidelines for bacteria and virus removal and provide safe drinking water to consumers without using any harmful chemicals."

Opportunity in Waste Streams

In the last chapter Frank Dulcich explained how Pacific Seafood looks for opportunities in its waste stream, a practice that has enabled the company to find a way to profit from the medical utility of a substance found in discarded shrimp shells. Dulcich makes it a point to encourage this kind of ingenuity in his company.

"If people just knew how much more money can be made if they're creative . . . " he muses. "I tell our people just to be curious. Maybe you don't know how to do it, but be curious and ask the questions to find out how we *can* do it. Don't tell me [that we can't do something]. I can always get somebody to tell me how we can't. We want to pay people to determine how we *can*."

Pacific Seafood found revenue in a resource that was being wasted. Aspen Skiing Company has displayed similar creativity by coming up with *two* clean-energy solutions in the last five or six years—both derived from sources that had previously gone untapped.

Aspen's president and CEO, Mike Kaplan, explained to me how this came about.

"So we do a fair amount of snowmaking on the mountains—probably eight hundred acres of snowmaking, and hundreds of millions of gallons of water every autumn up under the hill.

"Now, snowmakers are traditionally construction guys—you know, kind of cigarette-butt-in-the-mouth, running-the-backhoe kind of guys, right? And we had one guy—who recently passed away, actually—

named Jimmy Holton. Jimmy was just one of these guys. He never threw anything away; he was a scrap-it-together kind of guy.

"So, anyway, one day Jimmy said, 'You know, I'm not so sure about this environmental thing, but I can tell you, we got a lot of pipe and we got a lot of pressure up here. Don't you think those two things together could turn into hydropower?' And to make a long story short, he schemed up this idea of making a micro-hydro plant at Snowmass toward the bottom of the system. So they went and got the funding, and Jimmy Holton made it happen.

"This micro-hydro turbine captures a small percentage of the runoff that comes down the hill in the spring when our ponds get full, and it runs it through the pipe and we produce electricity through it."

As if this project weren't impressive enough in its inventiveness, Kaplan went on to tell me about yet another energy-related project his company is involved with: capturing methane from coal-mining operations and using it to generate electricity.

Methane is a dangerous byproduct of coal mining. The highly flammable gas must be vented from the mines for the safety of the miners, and this constitutes a problem for sustainability because methane is twenty[53] to twenty-five[54] times more potent a cause of global warming than CO_2. And when you consider that 40 percent of America's electricity comes from coal, the seriousness of the problem begins to become apparent.

Here's how it all came about, in Kaplan's words: "We [got involved through] an oil-and-gas engineer named Tom Vessels, who had learned about methane capture and its use in electricity generation in Europe. He identified the opportunity here in the States, especially in Colorado, where we have a number of very gassy coal mines that make a lot of

---

53   Bob Ward, "How Aspen Skiing Co. Became a Power Company," *The Aspen Times*, November 17, 2013

54   "Coal Mine Video, Aspen Skiing Company website: https://www.aspensnowmass.com/we-are-different/programs-and-practices

methane . . . and that methane is just being emitted into the atmosphere. It's a worker safety thing; you've got to vent the methane and not let the levels get too high. So he made a very sophisticated methane capture and venting system, but it was just releasing the gas into the atmosphere.

"We got introduced to Tom Vessels by the late Randy Udall, who was an energy guru and a great seeker of solutions to energy and climate challenges, and together, we approached our electricity provider, Holy Cross Energy, and we went to Elk Creek Mine to ask, 'Is there something we can do to help you turn this methane into electricity?' And everybody agreed, despite the fact that we totally disagreed on the reason why you would do it.

"Elk Creek Mine is owned by Bill Koch, the Oxbow Mining guy. We love them; they're down-to-earth, great guys. But when we start talking about climate science, it's like oil and water. I mean, we speak a different language, and those guys insist, 'No, the weather changes naturally. We can't change the weather, blah, blah, blah.' And they have their own charts and we've got our charts.

"But by the end of the day, we found common ground because neither of us liked to see a resource just going to waste. And they said that it's been driving them nuts for a while, because they spend so much time capturing it and they recognize that it's natural gas, and why wouldn't that get used, just as the coal they're mining gets used?

"I'm sure they also saw that it was good for business in other ways: *Hey, if we're being labeled as this dirty business, then if we can capture this methane and use it for electricity, that would be good for us from a regulatory standpoint and a PR standpoint.* So it's a story of people who could sit across the table and argue all day long and get nowhere, or find common ground and get something done. That benefits everybody.

"So, we put up three one-megawatt generators to capture that methane, and they're generating over twenty-four million kilowatt hours per year, which happens to be the equivalent of our annual electricity use, and it's actually three times our carbon emissions. And we're killing methane, pulling it out of the atmosphere and converting it to electricity."

Just to clarify the importance of what Kaplan is saying here, twenty-four million kilowatt hours per year is enough to power twenty-four hundred homes.

"We're pursuing more wide-scale investment in methane and trying to make it happen at a national level," Kaplan says, "because if business leaders weigh in, legislators start to listen."

I had some difficulty deciding whether to present Aspen Skiing Company's electricity-generating activities in this chapter or in the previous chapter about waste reduction. While both the hydroelectric generation from snow runoff and the recapture and use of methane from coal mining are perfect examples of a company identifying and seizing an opportunity to make money while performing a public service, they are also both perfect examples of our seventh best practice for sustainability: "Find Ways to Reduce Waste."

There are parallels to be found between Aspen Skiing Company's power generation and what Recology is doing in San Francisco. You may recall that Paul Polman said in the previous chapter, "If food waste were a country, it would be the third biggest climate emitter after China and the US." You may also recall that I mentioned how Recology collects organic waste by asking its restaurant customers to separate it from the rest of their trash. In doing this, Recology discovered an opportunity on which its giant competitors (as of this writing) are missing out.

I'll let Recology CEO Mike Sangiacomo tell you about this in his own words:

The City of San Francisco [encourages us to divert] organic waste to our composting program [with the understanding] that we will manufacture compost and sell it. [San Francisco is] a very urban environment, so we don't have a lot of yard waste. A typical suburban environment with recycling paper, bottles, cans, and yard trimmings could probably get very close to a 50 percent recycling or diversion rate. We didn't have that, so we said, "What are we going to do?"

So we did something called a *waste characterization study*. See what's in the waste stream. We knew we needed some data to be able to support the programs we wanted to propose, so we did this waste characterization study and found that the next two biggest things that we were still landfilling were construction waste and food waste. And we said, "Well we can build a facility to process construction waste," and we got approval. We did that and started diverting over 50 percent—and sometimes as much as 75 to 80 percent of the stuff that we were getting on the construction side—to beneficial reuse.

And then we scratched our heads. *So what do you do with used food?* And we said, "Let's try composting it!" So we went to some of our larger restaurant customers and said, "We want you to start separating your food waste, and we're going to compost it. We'll give you a little break on the garbage rate to warrant the extra work you have to do, but we really need you to help us work this out experimentally to see if it's going to work."

And we did that; we [experimented with the food waste until we were able to make] a really high-quality product. And so we got the city to buy in, and then we delivered a green waste bin to every business and resident in the city and said, "Please separate your organic matter in that bin." And now we take in close to seven hundred tons a day of organic matter to a compost facility to turn into a soil product that is alive; it has nutrient value in it, and good-quality bacteria that replenishes the soil, that adds nutrients and adds living matter to it that makes it healthier so that it grows better crops.

From my point of view, the benefits of keeping organics out of a landfill are significant in that you eliminate the creation of methane gas in landfills if there are no organic materials there. And it's a pretty nasty gas once it gets airborne, in terms of global warming.

We realized quite a few years ago, when we started down this path, that what we were doing was not just something that San Francisco wanted; other communities made it clear that they'd like [to have these kinds of programs] too, once they realized they worked. We were always looking at how we could compete as a small player in this industry; we're not puny, but Waste Management is thirteen or fourteen times our size. Republic Services is probably eight or nine times our size. How do we compete with companies like that, that own all this landfill capacity and make their money there? And we decided that if we can divert material from their landfills and find ways to make money for ourselves off it, then that has an impact on them. And they aren't going to compete very effectively in the communities that want the kinds of things that we've been able to do. Waste Management in particular is really hung up on maximizing profit, and they do that by landfilling. But [this can be a problem for them] if a city says, *We don't want you landfilling that stuff, and we can see it [being put to better use] in these other communities.* We're not the only ones doing this, but we're one of the bigger ones doing it. If it's possible in those other communities, why can't you do it? And if Waste Management won't do it for them, then they actually start to lose business.

And that has happened in all the states we operate in. In those states, they've lost business because communities have decided they don't want that model. Well, that has a beneficial impact for us because it gives us more opportunities to earn revenues and profits for ourselves. And we're winning business that used to be held by Waste Management, and some by Republic, as well.

Opportunity in Partnerships

Recology's activities are similar to Aspen Skiing Company's activities in a number of ways: both companies are finding ways to reduce methane pollution, and obviously, as I noted, both companies are finding revenue streams in waste products.

But there is a third similarity: both companies were creative in finding opportunities to partner with other entities (a practice whose importance we discussed in chapter 6). Aspen partnered with energy companies; Recology partnered with local governments and with *its own customers!* Perhaps one of the lessons here, to quote an old cliché, is that "One man's trash is another man's treasure" . . . and there's a lot of money to be made by finding a man whose trash is your treasure.

This maxim could almost be the motto of TerraCycle, a company devoted to "Eliminating the Idea of Waste®" by recycling the 'non-recyclable.'"[55] Tom Szaky, TerraCycle's founder, explained to me how his company's business model works, and how it partners with other businesses:

"Maybe the best way to start is to ask, 'What is our purpose as a business?' So TerraCycle has been around for thirteen years. We have enjoyed straight growth on all metrics since launch, and we now operate in twenty countries around the world. We are actually launching in three more this year or next, depending on how fast we get there.

---

55   TerraCycle website: https://www.terracycle.com/en-US/

"Now, what we do as a company is probably the more important aspect of who we are. We focus on making things recyclable that are not recyclable, and in order to understand that statement, it is important to understand why something is recyclable or is not recyclable. So, just looking around my desk, I have a recyclable object and a non-recyclable one. Let's just say this glass jar is highly recyclable everywhere in the world, yet this pen is not recyclable anywhere in the world, and the first question is *why*.

"The reason is that the cost of collecting this jar and processing it is less than the value retained when you sell the resulting glass; so you can make money, and that is why companies get into that business. While the pen, on the other hand, can technically be recycled. It costs more to collect and process than it is worth, which is why in no country in the world it is recycled.

"So what TerraCycle does is, we find partners. We have been successful in five different areas: one is with big consumer-product companies; retailers are the second; third, manufacturing facilities or distribution centers; fourth, cities; and fifth, individuals or small businesses. We engage these constituents in funding that economic delta, which allows us then to make that object nationally recyclable.

"TerraCycle has no direct competition anywhere in the world. There is no company that does what we do. So in most of these cases, we are going in and opening a whole new perspective for folks, because many of these companies never thought that their products could be recycled before. For example, we invented cigarette recycling three years ago, and we work now with every major tobacco company on the planet. But if you'd talked to these tobacco companies before we came around, none of them thought that it was even possible to recycle a cigarette butt."

Szaky gave me an example of one of TerraCycle's successful partnerships—an arrangement with Staples to run an in-store program to recycle notebook binders. TerraCycle benefits from this arrangement by acquiring material for its manufacturing needs; Staples benefits because the program drives foot traffic into the store.

"The best way to communicate—if you are talking to a retailer, for example—is that it is not about sustainability; it is about how we drive foot traffic to your store.

"So we work with Staples in the US to recycle binders, and in Canada to recycle pens. So now you can go to any Staples store in either of those countries and take either of those waste streams in to be recycled. That is the platform.

"So, it would be a cost to Staples in the US to have the binders recycled because it costs more to collect and process them than the resulting paper, metal, and plastic is worth. The primary reason Staples likes this is that more people will come into the store. Why? Because they are bringing their binders back into the store. It is that simple and concrete: a consumer wants to recycle her binder, looks it up, finds that she can do it at Staples, and physically gets into her car and drives it in, and drops it off in the bin. And that is valuable to Staples because when someone enters their store, there is a chance that that person will become a consumer of theirs and buy their office supplies at Staples and not from a competitor.

"Secondary to that is the PR value, the marketing value, the fact that there is a good social mission that can show up in the CSR report. But the primary value, the main decision-making value is how many more people come into the store because of this.

"The real question was getting them to overcome the initial doubt—would anyone even *want* this? Would it work? The key question Staples had was, "Would people pay to recycle something when they can throw it out for free?" The big concern was this unknown. The service has never existed. Is there a market? A lot of retailers, when we pitched this to them, initially said no because they thought that there was no way there would be a market. Staples took the leap and listed it, and it became a very high revenue-generating platform for them. It then moved into the US, and it has been a landmark success and now it is being replicated by other retailers."

Key Takeaways

1. Adaptability and the ability to recognize opportunity are essential for success in any business (and in every other aspect of life).
2. Big social changes (such as the rise of the Internet, for example) almost always present such opportunities.
3. Even the very poor are potential customers.
4. Opportunity lurks even in your trash (or someone else's).
5. A willingness to form partnerships opens up additional opportunities.

→ CHAPTER 9 ←

MEASURE THE RETURN ON SUSTAINABILITY INVESTMENT

"Every line is the perfect length if you don't measure it."
—**Marty Rubin**, author of *The Boiled Frog Syndrome*

What gets measured gets done. That is a fundamental tenet of business management. By developing methods to measure the impact of our investments of time and money into sustainability, we are able to see whether we are making progress or need to course-correct. And key metrics in the area of sustainability are evolving even as you read this.

The benefits of these metrics are twofold:

1. To manage the progress of the teams working on these initiatives and make course corrections if the desired results aren't being achieved

2. To show investors what the tangible returns are on the investment

These metrics can also serve as an inspiration for the general population, showing them what is being done and encouraging them to get involved as well (which will be the subject of our now-imminent final chapter).

The previous chapters in this book abound with examples of measurement as a best practice for global sustainability. Recall, for example, that in the discussion about waste reduction in chapter 7, Pacific Seafood's Frank Dulcich said, "By continually monitoring and improving our work processes, our cook techniques, and our harvest techniques, we now are able to achieve double the protein return from the same animal." This improvement to Pacific's processes enabled them to reduce the environmental impact of their fishing activity by 50 percent with no loss in the amount of food produced, and it was made possible by measurement—without which, they would never have discovered the inefficiency in the first place.

Another good example would be the waste characterization study that Recology undertook in San Francisco: had Recology not been motivated to look into the contents of the waste they were managing, they would have missed out on the revenue stream they found in the city's compostable food waste.

Tata—Measuring the Success of Volunteering and Job-Training Programs

As I mentioned in chapter 1, the Tata group runs various programs to encourage volunteerism among their employees. Tata's chief ethics officer, Dr. Mukund Rajan, told me a bit about how Tata measures and quantifies the success of these programs.

"We have a dedicated team that really pursues this agenda. I think a big part of what they do is communication, and another part of it is measurement. You know the old adage: 'What gets measured is what gets improved.' So we try to get feedback [from the companies involved in this program] about the kind of impact our volunteers have, and then each year, the benchmark is set a little higher.

"So let me just give you three illustrations of the way measurement and improvement take place. The first is with the episodic Tata volunteering weeks. Here, we measure how many volunteering hours our people are able to contribute. There is obviously a structure and a process followed by the team that coordinates all this, which is really to encourage companies to coordinate and to curate the right kinds of volunteering projects. So companies are able to post the volunteering projects that they would be supporting across different cities, all across the world, and companies then cascade that information to their employees, and people can sign up for whatever holds their interest.

"What we also do at the end of the volunteering weeks is undertake a survey of the employees to see how they really responded to the opportunities. Was it the first time they did it or have they done it before? Would they do it again? And I think the beautiful thing about taking that feedback from the employees has been that typically 99 percent—and that's not a made-up number; that's actually the response that we got—said it was something that they felt in some ways even changed their lives.

"We've taken a lot of support from the Tata Trusts in identifying the right nonprofits to work with on pro bono projects. Because initially, we felt it's important to ensure that we work with organizations that have credibility, that have already had significant impact on the ground. It's a two-way measure. We ask the employees how they rate the nonprofit in the project, and we also ask the nonprofit how they rate the contribution the employees have made. So those are some of the ways in which we really try and assess the efficacy of what we are doing in the volunteering space."

Tata also carefully monitors the progress of its STRIVE program for vocational training (described in chapter 2). I asked Dr. Rajan whether the company had developed any metrics for this purpose.

"Yes," he said. "This will be our first year of the Skill Development Initiative, and some of the metrics are related to the kinds of people that we're able to put through the Skill Development Program.

"So in India we have what are referred to as the scheduled caste and scheduled tribe communities; some of the most underprivileged communities in society. So we're looking at what percentage of the people who are put through the Skill Development Program come from those communities. We are also tracking how many are women, with a view to the diversity agenda. And then we want to make sure that as many as possible of the people who go through our program are employed for a period of time, so you want to track how long they stay in jobs because that'll be the real measure of the value of the Skill Development Program; if they can stay employed and they're not either fired or driven to quit out of frustration.

"We're trying to use Information Technology to the fullest; in fact, a large part of the team that runs the Tata STRIVE program actually has been loaned to the Initiative pro bono by Tata Consultancy Services, which is helping to both manage the platform on which we collect all the data for the candidates and ensure that each candidate has a unique ID. But this'll be the first year of the program, so I think the proof of concept will really come in the subsequent years."

Kering and Natura—Measuring Environmental Profit & Loss

In chapter 6 I mentioned Kering's E P&L tool, a subject that came up when I asked Kering CEO François-Henri Pinault whether Kering had metrics in place to let them know that they're getting a return on their sustainability investment.

The purpose of the E P&L is to increase a company's understanding of the environmental impact of their business. E P&L analysis measures the impact of a company's operations—on its supply chain, on the environment, on the communities in which the company does business, and so forth—and assigns a monetary value to that impact.[56] When I asked him for more information, Pinault provided me with a wealth of information about Environmental Profit & Loss.

"When we started, we didn't have [these kinds of metrics], but as we were going forward, we realized that we really needed a consistent way to measure our achievement and make sure that we were improving the situation of the company. We spent four or five years working on a project that we released last year, which is the Environmental Profit & Loss—E P&L. We were the first group in the world to release a full, consolidated E P&L, which means that every brand of my group—and I have twenty brands—is releasing, every year, an E P&L based on the methodology that we created with the help of partners, audit firms, and some NGOs that were involved with us.

"We were the beta tester of the E P&L, and this is the ultimate tool for us to set the starting points and make sure that, year after year, we are improving, but more important, that we are working through a set of priorities that is meaningful at the group level—meaning that we realize, for instance, that if we were to consider sustainability issues only in our legal boundaries, we would have addressed only 7 percent of our global carbon footprint.

---

56   Kering website: http://www.kering.com/en/sustainability/epl

"And the E P&L showed us that 93 percent of our carbon footprint was outside my legal boundaries, along the supply chains in my different businesses. So it's very important that, in light of this, you set the right priorities to make sure that you're moving in the right direction at the group level and also at the brand level."

In accordance with the best practice of collaboration and partnership discussed in chapter 6, Kering has shared this tool with the world at large . . . and other companies are using it. One such company is Natura, which has worked to develop its own E P&L methodology. Natura's co-chairman, Guilherme Leal, described to me his company's efforts to measure the results of their investments in sustainability.

"A major challenge here is to measure and put financial value on both our negative and positive externalities, and this is why we are developing the E P&L, as I mentioned. We have also joined a group of companies, including Kering and Unilever, led by the WBCSD [the *World Business Council for Sustainable Development*], to create an international protocol for the E P&L, the Natural Capital Protocol, that should be easily replicable and scalable. We plan to have a similar methodology for measuring our social impacts, the S P&L [Social Profit & Loss], and we'll start working on it this year.

"We believe deeply that markets are the best way to allocate efforts to promote the quality of life in society. But we deal with imperfect markets. The social and environmental impacts are not considered in our costs. So while we think that the markets are still the best way to promote progress, we need to perfect them. We need to incorporate into our price system the other impacts that are being paid for and distributed in an unfair way among the different people around the world.

"So we think that to bring and to build an environmental P&L and social P&L it's key. It's tough; it's a pilot. We are a part of this natural capital coalition led by the World Business Council, IUCN [the International Union for Conservation of Nature], and other institutions that are trying, through those experiences and with the support of PricewaterhouseCoopers (PwC), to create a pilot of measurement that could be shared with other companies.

"We are just finishing our first P&L measure, and this next month, those results are supposed to be made public. It's a novelty and it's tough to build, but we try always to be part of this leadership and to experience new things. But we cannot measure our advancements without tools appropriate to this work.

"As you know, Kering has been doing important work on this, and they are somewhat advanced in relation to Natura. But we have a wider spectrum to consider—the extraction of the raw materials and the discarding of the products. So our spectrum is a little wider compared to Kering, but they were an inspiration for us, and the idea is to be working together, not only with Kering, but with this whole coalition."

> *"We do a sustainability report every two years. We count our emissions against our targets and we sort of try to daylight wins and losses—what's worked and what hasn't. We set those goals through the climate action plan and hold ourselves accountable to those."*
> —**Mike Kaplan**, president and CEO, Aspen Skiing Company

Guidance—Measuring Employee Commutes

Guidance founder Jon Provisor feels strongly about reducing his company's carbon footprint, and he understands that the only way to do that is to take measurements of that footprint.

"About ten years ago we created what we call the Guidance Green Committee. So the first step was internally optimize our own systems in every possible way. We measured our carbon expenditure, we measured travel, we measured commutes, and we encouraged carpooling. We have an award every month for the greenest person in terms of travel. Did they ride, did they walk, or did they take a bus, versus having their five-thousand-pound car transport them twenty-five miles [to Marina del Rey] from the San Fernando Valley? So, we enlightened people to look at how they travel. We have a bike-to-work day, and we encourage everyone to bike to work; or if you are too far away, at least to carpool to work. Once a year we do that."

Of course the results of a program like this have to be measurable if it is to do any good. Provisor explained to me how Guidance goes about measuring its energy use and carbon output. "Our financial department devotes some time to looking at our air travel and calculating the carbon related to that. We look at our energy bills and we offset our energy. We have a carbon spreadsheet that we leverage with all travel, transportation, and energy expenditures, and then we offset that with carbon credits. So we have tried to look at every single element of energy usage in the company—computers, monitors, servers, copiers, refrigerators, and dishwashers—and to optimize them as much as possible with the most efficient systems."

Unilever's Paul Polman on Measurement

"We look at many indicators. We look at how many people we reached that year for health and well-being, and how much more we are sustainably sourced, and increasingly, the financial market appreciates that. Our share price last year alone was up again 12 percent. If you add dividends with it, it is nearly 30 percent. So it has more than doubled over the last six or seven years, but we are not short-circuiting anybody, and increasingly, the financial market understands that. They understand that companies that operate with more transparency—and that internalize some of these external challenges—are companies that are probably better managed and run a lower risk. And with a lower risk comes a lower cost of capital and a higher return, and increasingly, the financial data show it.

"For Unilever, our overarching measures are our positive social impact and the decoupling of our growth from our environmental impact. We measure that by making all our agriculturally-based raw materials sustainable. We had around 10 percent five years ago, and now we're at 60 percent. So you can unlock some things."

Seth Goldman: Keeping Honest Tea *Honest*

In 2008 the Coca-Cola Company made a 40 percent investment in Honest Tea, and in 2011 it bought the company outright. Naturally, there was concern about how this acquisition by such a corporate giant would look to Honest Tea's customer base, many of whom are loyal to Honest Tea because of its ideals and its sustainability-oriented mission. Seth Goldman explained to me how this was handled, and why it was important to handle it properly.

"Well, the first thing we have to do—and I believe other companies need to do this if they're serious about this—you have to hold yourself accountable. So there's no question that we'll move around from year to year in terms of what we'll invest in, but every year we need to be reporting to our employees and to other stakeholders about where we're investing our efforts.

"So in 2008 we came out with our first mission report. And, of course, Coca-Cola invested in us in 2008, and at that time we realized that although we were still committed to our mission, we weren't reporting on it annually. But now that we're part of a larger company, we need to continue to be transparent. And we can't expect consumers to give us the benefit of the doubt.

"So we said, 'Let's start being accountable.' We started putting together an annual mission report, and we were very conscious about it not being a cheerleading document. It's not about patting ourselves on the back for saving the world. It is being transparent about where we're making our investments. Where we're succeeding. Where we're failing.

What more we have to do. Where something didn't work out. That transparency is really important, and I think that often companies will put out what they'll call a CSR [corporate social responsibility] report, and it's often put out by the marketing department. But for us, this is a core part of our business."

Standardization of Global Sustainability Measurements

"*The new SASB standards allow us—for the first time—to identify and measure exposure to climate risk across companies and industries. Climate change affects all markets and presents risks that investors can no longer ignore. The standards help them understand their exposure while also directing capital to the strongest performing companies.*"

—**Michael Bloomberg**, chairman,
Sustainability Accounting Standards Board

One of the overarching themes of this book is that investment in global sustainability is not just good for the planet and the people who live on it, but also good for business—and therefore, sustainable from a business perspective. But while I feel that I've provided ample illustrations of this, it's not quite enough just to make the claim. The results have to be quantifiable. They have to be *measurable*.

Fortunately, others besides me have also come to this conclusion and have set themselves to the task of finding objective ways to measure the results of sustainability commitments. The partnership described earlier in this chapter comprising Kering, Natura, the World Business Council, IUCN, and other entities is one example of such an effort.

Another example can be found in the work of a nonprofit organization known as the Sustainability Accounting Standards Board (SASB). "Material information is the right of every investor," says

SASB CEO Jean Rogers. "In order to get a full picture of corporate performance, investors need to be able to type in a ticker and access sustainability fundamentals right alongside financial fundamentals."

Writing about SASB in *Forbes*, Dr. Bob Eccles says, "What the world needs now, in addition to love, sweet love, is accounting standards for measuring so-called 'nonfinancial performance,' i.e., how well a company is performing on the environmental, social, and governance (ESG) issues that are important to investors. For without these standards, we won't have the capital markets we need today to create a sustainable society for future generations.

"While the role of standards for both financial and nonfinancial information is the same—to help investors make their resource allocation decisions—there is an important difference. The ESG issues that must be properly managed in order to create value over the long term—or what is called "material" in the language of corporate reporting—vary by industry. A chemical company's carbon emissions are more material to that organization than say, to a bank."[57]

SASB has therefore devised a ten-sector classification system, subdivided into seventy-nine separate industries, and identified 1) what sustainability issues are likely to be relevant to each industry and 2) the appropriate Key Performance Indicators (KPIs) that would serve as metrics to enable a company to report on its progress in these areas. These metrics will enable investors to evaluate a company's commitment to global sustainability, and to understand how that commitment affects the company's financial performance.

With access to tools such as this—not to mention Kering's E P&L and other apparatuses—investors, business leaders, and the general public now have the wherewithal to find a way forward, a way to balance the once-irreconcilable exigencies of clean air, social justice, and

---

57 Dr. Bob Eccles, "What The World Needs Now: Sustainability Accounting Standards," *Forbes*, May 3, 2016

economic necessity. And in our next and final chapter, I'll outline what you can do to contribute to the more livable world that awaits us in the not-too-distant future.

Key Takeaways

1. What gets measured gets done.
2. In order for a significant investment in GS to be sustainable for a business, investors have to be able to understand how that investment affects the company's financial performance.
3. Sustainability measurements are potentially as important as financial data.
4. Collaboration with other businesses improves the metrics by which we measure the success of GS practices.
5. Measurement often brings new business opportunities to light.

CHAPTER 10

CONCLUSION AND CALL TO ACTION

"The best time to plant a tree was twenty years ago. The next best time is today."

—Chinese Proverb

I n the pages of this book I've covered a number of different topics related to global sustainability—poverty, hunger, the environment, etc. The problems we face in each of these areas are separate concerns, but they are nonetheless connected: for example, deforestation and bad farming practices in underdeveloped countries cause hunger and poverty—and poverty is one cause of social unrest and warfare, which, in turn, help to perpetuate poverty.

Our reasons for being concerned about these problems are twofold: compassion and self-interest. We care (or *should* care) about the well-being of other human beings simply because, like us, they *are* human beings. But even if our shared humanity were not reason enough to concern ourselves with these problems, it would still be in our interest to attempt to mitigate them. Prosperous societies are viable consumer markets; malnourished and impoverished communities cannot buy the goods we produce. Political violence and instability are likewise bad for business. And underlying all these concerns is the environment; fishing and agribusiness depend on our ability to put back into ecosystems as much as we take out of them, and on our ability to operate without poisoning the wells from which we drink. This is one reason why companies like Dow and DSM hold themselves to high environmental standards, even when operating in countries where they are not required to do so. It is also part of the reason Cargill teaches rural farmers to farm sustainably, and the reason Pacific Seafood takes care to minimize the environmental impact of its fishing operations.

The UN's Seventeen Sustainable Development Goals

In the first few pages of this book I described the United Nations' Sustainable Development Goals for 2030, which have been agreed upon by 193 countries:

1. Ending poverty
2. Ending hunger
3. Ensuring universal health and well being
4. Ensuring universal access to quality education
5. Achieving gender equality
6. Ensuring universal access to clean water and sanitation
7. Ensuring universal access to affordable, reliable, sustainable, and modern energy
8. Promoting inclusive and sustainable economic growth so that decent work is available to everyone

9. Building resilient infrastructure and promoting sustainable industrialization

10. Reducing economic inequality within and among countries

11. Making cities inclusive and safe

12. Ensuring sustainable consumption and production patterns (i.e., reducing food and energy waste)

13. Combating climate change

14. "Life below Water": Protecting the oceans and ensuring the sustainability of marine resources

15. "Life on Land": Sustainably managing forests, combating desertification, halting and reversing land degradation, and halting the loss of biodiversity

16. Promoting just, peaceful, and inclusive societies

17. Revitalizing the global partnership for sustainable development (i.e., ensuring continued cooperation among different governments in order to achieve these goals)

The common thread uniting the companies whose leaders have contributed their thoughts and their time to the writing of this book—from relatively small businesses like TerraCycle to global behemoths like Unilever—is their commitment to supporting these goals.

The Dow Chemical Company

Shortly before I interviewed The Dow Chemical Company's CEO Andrew Liveris, the company thoughtfully provided me with a document detailing what Dow considers to be the Best Practices for Global Sustainability, and which of the UN's seventeen Sustainable Development Goals it considers most relevant to its business. Reading this document, I was delighted to learn how seriously Dow takes these issues.

Dow is taking action to address each of these sustainability goals. When the UN SDGs were launched in September 2015, the UN Foundation asked companies to commit to three to five goals that most likely aligned to their innovations, core competencies, and products. Dow chose to focus most on advancing the following goals:

Goal 2: Zero Hunger
Goal 6: Clean Water and Sanitation
Goal 9: Infrastructure and Innovation
Goal 15: Life on Land
Goal 17: Partnerships for the Goals

Reading further, I found that Dow is quite proud of the results they've achieved with their interest in sustainability.

"Not only do our efforts earn us the right to operate on this planet; they are also a critical element of our business strategy. Take China, for example, where Dow's focus on delivering sustainable value enabled us to grow volume by 10 percent last quarter."

When I spoke to Andrew Liveris, he described Dow's sustainability activities in more detail (as you've already read), but expressed some disappointment in the degree to which the rest of the world has followed suit, saying, "I do think we are failing collectively as a society to integrate the principles of the United Nations and the SDG 17."

Natura

When I asked Natura co-chairman Guilherme Leal about the UN's goals, he was happy to tell me about Natura's adoption of them, and about how Natura was already ahead of the UN on some issues.

"We have just made an assessment last year," Leal told me, "and found out that Natura contributes somehow to fifteen of the seventeen

Sustainable Development Goals through its policies, practices, and corporate culture. For example, Natura is a pioneer in sharing the benefits of biodiversity with traditional communities in the Amazon, helping to generate income and fight poverty in the region. Last year we also adopted the Social Progress Index created by Michael Porter to assess human and social development in these communities and increase their well-being. This was an important step for us, as the concern about the social impact of our business has always been part of Natura's essence."

Unilever

"What we are trying to do is link each of our brands to these main goals and bring these brands' purposes more to life by contributing to the goals," says Paul Polman. "So, for example, our Knorr® brand, obviously, is food and food security. It is a very clear link. Our bar-soap brands like Lifebuoy work on sanitation; there is a specific sub-goal in there relating to handwashing. A brand like Domestos is working on installing toilets and ending the issue of open defecation.[58]

"Even a brand like Dove works on women's self-esteem, which has a separate goal in there relating to gender equality, which is goal number five. So all of our brands have a clear mission and a clear vision of how they contribute to the goals.

"So you take health and hygiene; the commitment we have made to reach a billion people, that goes to goal number six, which is about clean water and sanitation. If you have a product like we have, like Pureit, the water purifier, it contributes to clean water, but we also have it in many other parts of our operations. All our factories need to have clean water, and need to use less water.

---

58 Open defecation is the practice of defecating outdoors rather than into a toilet. It is rampant in poor countries that lack adequate sanitation infrastructure, and poses a severe public-health problem in such places. http://unicef.in/ Whatwedo/11/Eliminate-Open-Defecation

"If you have a [company] goal relating to fairness in the workplace, then it gets to goal number five on gender equality, or goal number eight, which is about decent work and opportunity for all. So every initiative that we have, every brand that we have, we link to a dominant goal, but it also will have spinoffs on other goals. So we approach all these brands from an angle of all the SDGs and make the Unilever Sustainable Living Plan our overall umbrella to make these SDGs come alive."

Setting an Example

"A big part of our effort is external. We could shut down tomorrow and close every lift and close every building and get to carbon zero, right? But is that going to stop climate change? No. It's not even going to have an impact. But if we could serve as a model and influence others to do more and create a movement, and influence our legislators to act, then maybe we can actually solve this problem. So it's not about the awards and looking good to the press. It's about trying to win this because it's an imminent and tangible threat to our livelihood."
—**Mike Kaplan**, president and CEO, Aspen Skiing Company

If we are to make the necessary changes to our society that will enable us to sustain our standard of living and extend it across the globe, it is not enough to preach the gospel of global sustainability; we must also practice it. No one takes advice or orders from a fraud or a hypocrite.

In his time at The Dow Chemical Company, Andrew Liveris has built an impressive legacy of sustainability-as-business-strategy—a legacy he doesn't intend to neglect after he retires from his current position (which he plans to do as soon as he finishes midwifing Dow's imminent merger with DuPont).

"I think the platform matters," he says, "and being CEO of a publicly held large corporation obviously gives me a great platform. And once we complete this merger, I will go find every platform I can. I will write a book. I will go to join think tanks. And I will join NGO boards. I will go to schools and be a volunteer teacher. I will go to campuses and help MBA students. I play on the field; I don't play in the grandstands."

Kering's François-Henri Pinault says he began to see the importance of setting a corporate example after he started getting involved with sustainability in 2007 in partnership with Jochen Zeitz, who was CEO of Puma at that time.

"I said to Jochen, 'I'm not doing this for any communication reason.' But eventually, I realized that I have also another responsibility that I didn't see at that time, which is to set an example for my peers.

"I'm also the main shareholder of my company. It's a family business. So it gives me more room to move and to convince the financial markets of the strategy we're putting in place. It's also a set of responsibilities that I endorsed three or four years ago, when I decided to communicate what I was doing, our different achievements, to publically set our targets; by the way, we publish, each year, our achievements that we set in 2012 for 2016, and we will release at the end of this year our target for 2025. We do that not for image purposes, but to set an example and to try to influence our peers in a positive way."

Salesforce and the 1-1-1 Model

Salesforce is well known for its unique philanthropic venture, Pledge 1%, also known as the 1-1-1 Philanthropic Model. The idea is that 1 percent of any company's time, product, or resources is an easy amount to give (1 percent of an average workday, for example, is about five minutes), and if everyone did so, substantial progress could be made toward making the world a better place—which, in turn, would go a long way toward furthering the UN's seventeen Sustainable Development Goals. To this end, Salesforce created Salesforce.org, a nonprofit entity that donates 1 percent of Salesforce's equity, time, and product to good causes. The company encourages other businesses and wealthy individuals to do the same by pledging to donate 1 percent of their product, 1 percent of their time, or 1 percent of their equity to organizations that are working to improve the world in some substantial way.[59]

I asked Salesforce CEO Marc Benioff to explain the 1-1-1 Model to me in greater detail, and to describe its origin.

"I worked at Oracle for many years," he said, "and as I was finishing up my career there, I realized that I kind of had a false choice: the idea that I was either going to have to work inside a company or do nonprofit work [but couldn't do both]. And when I was doing nonprofit work as part of Oracle, we had a really sentimental experience putting computers into schools, but employees just were not that excited about it because they didn't view it as part of our culture or as something the CEO was committed to.

"So when I started Salesforce, I wanted to make sure that I created a model that allowed employees to do nonprofit work as powerfully as if they were doing work in the company. And I wanted to bring all the company's resources, relationships, and even finances to bear to support the communities where we live and work, and that's where the 1-1-1 Model came from. We took 1 percent of our equity, our product, and our time and we started a charity so that we could scale our ability to do good wherever we went.

"And that's worked out really well. Today we've given more than $100 million in grants, we've done more than one and a half million hours of volunteerism, and we run more than twenty-eight thousand nonprofits and NGOs for free on our service. But more important than that, more than 90 percent of our employees participate in our seven days' paid time off for volunteerism. That's the real power."

---

59 http://www.salesforce.org/pledge-1/

Unilever

Unilever's Paul Polman understands very well that the value of the good work his company does lies not in the public approbation and resultant good PR, nor in how good it may make him feel personally, but in the size of the fire he is able to light by setting an example.

"Through our handwashing programs, we have reached nearly 350 million people," he says, "and we are trying to reach a billion people. We are moving whole markets now to sustainable agriculture. I have always said that I am proud of what Unilever does, and we try to do more, but if at the end of the day, it is only Unilever that does that, and nobody else does, then we have failed miserably. So we need to be sure that we are not too far ahead, and we need to be sure that we use our value-chain reach and our size and scale to drive these tipping points in the whole industry in these different areas that are important to us.

"We also encourage and incentivize our senior managers to invest a short-term compensation into the long-term so that they become bigger shareholders and put their money where their mouths are. So there are different things that we do to drive behavior that some people like and other people, perhaps don't, but we have a big enough critical mass of people who like that, so that supports our philosophy. I cannot be in Paris and talk about climate change and be seen as one of the major proponents of an agreement if I, myself, behave irresponsibly. That is why I have solar panels on my roof and double windows and LED lights and I have made my house carbon neutral. So you live what you preach, and we give the people in the company that opportunity to be part of that."

DSM's Feike Sijbesma feels keenly the responsibility to live out the public position he has taken on sustainability, and he doesn't mince words when talking about those who don't.

"For ten years [I have attended] the World Economic Forum, and one of the first times I was there, a former head of state—I will not mention his name—told a brilliant story about sustainability and values and seeing the future, etc. It was very inspirational. I'll never forget it. And after the applause, a lady sitting next to me said to this person, 'It's great what you did. Really, it's inspirational.' And he was smiling, feeling great about being acknowledged. And then she finished by saying, 'It's a pity that when you really had the power as a head of state, you never talked about this. You did nothing about this. But it is great that since you are retired, now you talk about all this stuff.'

"He was pissed off, and he said, 'Yeah, but I needed to operate in a coalition and it was not easy for me,' and so on. And I thought, *Well, I don't work [in government], but I work also in coalitions.* And if I only advocate all these things when I'm retired, I will not be able to look in the eyes of my children. I mean, that is a coward's behavior. If I have an opinion on this and I have a vision—and I do—then [I had] better do it when I am in charge. Do I take a risk? Yes. Is it easier to grow only for the short term in this financial environment? Absolutely. Would I have then an easier life with some stakeholders? Absolutely. Is that wrong? I think so. Is that a misuse of the impact that I can have? I would think so."

Global Sustainability Investment Is Good for Business . . . But What if It Weren't?

> *"Sustainability is when our love for our children is stronger than our greed for our own well-being."*
> —**Paul Polman**, CEO, Unilever

It's easy to get carried away with the potential return on an investment in sustainability, but it's important to remember that this is ultimately not the most pressing reason to embrace the idea. I've made over and over again the point that sustainability-related practices are good for business, and I believe—and all the CEOs I spoke to also believe—that it *has* to be economically viable if it's going to work. If our environmental and political needs were not reconcilable with the laws of economics, then we might all be doomed.

BUT . . . the stakes are too high to hold sustainability practices to the promise of maximum profitability at all times, in all situations. A worldwide embrace of the best practices for global sustainability is necessary for the long-term survival of our economy and our society, and, ultimately, our very lives. Global sustainability may indeed be good for business, but it would be necessary even if it were not.

Perhaps because he is in the food-production business, the seriousness of this matter is not lost on Cargill's David MacLennan.

"We're making food," he says, "and we're making the world a better place and helping nourish the planet and doing it in a responsible way. But it's also a challenge: when we signed the UN's New York Declaration on Forests in 2014, one of our business leaders called and said, 'You know this is going to cost me a lot of money to do this in terms of buying only from farmers who do not grow in deforested land.' And I said, 'I know you believe it's going to cost you money, but I think ultimately, it's going to lead to greater profitability because this is where the world is going. This is what is expected of large companies like ours.'

"And so it must be integrated as part of the business model. And how do you sell it to your shareholders with respect to profitability and return? I have no doubt because I've talked to them about it. But the legacy of this company and of its family owners is over 151 years in the business, and as owners, they want to do things the right way, with respect for the planet and with respect for resources—and most important, with respect for people, helping to make their lives better. And [the family is] happy to invest their earnings and lower their returns if that's what it takes to do that. So there is complete support and buy-in. It's just part of the family-owned shareholder culture and ethos.

I asked MacLennan if there were a theoretical parameter that the family shareholders might use in making that judgment, whereby they could say, "We're willing to address 10 percent or 20 percent, or we're willing to pay a premium or realize a reduced return by X percent as a contribution for this."

"No," he replied. "I don't think they'd want to do that because then, in some ways, you're putting a value on human life and human livelihood and nourishment. I think over time, if our returns were to drop and I said, well, you know, 4 percent of our returns—I'm just making up a number now—are because of sustainability, I don't think they'd balk. They're not the kind of people who are going to say 'We're going to do it, but only up to a certain point.' I think they expect us to incorporate sustainability into our business model, but to do it in a way that doesn't dramatically decrease profits. I don't believe they would set up parameters.

"Yes, there's a cost to investing in sustainability, but we will pay for it in other ways; we will find efficiencies in other areas to pay for this. I always believe there's ways to invest in and pay for the things you find most important. So I wouldn't accept a decline in profitability being blamed on sustainability.

"I think sustainability is catching on. I see more and more of our competitors, more and more of the industry doing it. Companies' reputations are affected favorably or negatively relative to how they're handling it. I think the pace of expectation and the pace of change as it relates to sustainability is only going to increase. So I think there's a great opportunity for those who are committed to it, and I think if you're not, then you're going to be playing catch-up."

"Sustainability is an integrated business driver. It is doing good, doing well, doing well by doing good, and having the right outcomes."
—**Andrew Liveris**, CEO, The Dow Chemical Company

Richard Branson also feels that commitment to sustainability is both necessary for human survival and necessary for business in the long run. In chapter 6 we learned about Branson's involvement with The Elders, the group founded by Nelson Mandela to address the global problem of armed conflict. When we got deeper into the subject, Branson— displaying the optimism that is one of his more charming qualities— told me why he feels it's necessary for business leaders to step up to the proverbial plate:

"OK, Syria has obviously been a complete nightmare, but if you take Syria and ISIS out of the equation just for a minute, every decade for the last fifty years, the world is generally getting better and better and better.

"The Millennium Development Goals were tremendous, and there was a lot of cynicism about them at the time, but a lot has been achieved from these Goals. More people are being pulled out of poverty every decade; we're talking hundreds of millions of new people coming out of the poverty trap.

"But there is still a ton of work to do, and I think, in the past, businesses sort of thought, *OK, we're running our businesses; we'll leave governments to deal with these social issues.* I think, in the last ten years, more and more businesses have begun to think that they can play a much bigger role in sorting out the problems of the world, rather than just leaving it to government and the social sects to do that, and I see businesspeople who have particular skills that politicians and social workers sometimes don't have."

"*We need to generate economic value while at the same time, generate environmental value and societal value. We call that the triple bottom line, and it is what we need to do. Creating environmental and societal value is a primary goal of the company*

itself as well—not a secondary goal, but a primary goal next to economic value."
—**Feike Sijbesma**, CEO, DSM

On the necessity of global sustainability, regardless of whether it's good for business, TerraCycle's Tom Szaky takes a harder, more unforgiving line than most of the CEOs with whom I spoke.

"Most organizations are focused on sustainability where it drives business value," he says, "but I think the real thing we need to be celebrating is not people who do that, but rather, the organizations—which are few and far between—that focus on sustainability even where it may harm the business. Because at the end of the day, you can't grow consumption and then somehow wake up on a better planet. It just can't happen. So the case studies I really look for (which are also few and far between) are the ones in which a company takes a critical look and maybe makes a very difficult decision in the name of sustainability. Because if an action is taken in the name of sustainability and drives profit, then that only goes so far, and I feel like we put too much focus on rewarding companies for doing the latter rather than the former."

A Call to Action

If you've read this far, it's safe to assume that you're interested in sustainability and want to do what you can to contribute to it. Hopefully, the steps and practices I've outlined in these pages are enough to get you started on that path, and who knows—perhaps something you've come across here will inspire the next game-changing great idea.

Beyond minding these principles and practices, there are a couple of other things you can do:

Be Conscious

You will recall that in the "Invitation" chapter of this book, I discussed the concept of *conscious leadership*, which depends on our awareness that we have the ability to have an impact, and that whatever we do has an impact on everything. Seth Goldman of Honest Tea sums up conscious leadership beautifully.

"Obviously, the UN goals resonate. They're really at the core of our business, and even more broadly now that I'm involved with multiple companies. Human beings obviously are the most immediate group that we think about our impact on. But how we source our ingredients has an impact on the planet as well. The plants are part of that ecosystem as well. If you're committed to the idea of sustaining and upholding life, and yet you operate in a consumer economy . . . the definition of *consume* by the dictionary is to devour and destroy.

"So we all live in this contradiction, and I think there's no such thing as a socially responsible company that doesn't have a consumption component to it. So how do you reconcile that? I think the first step is to understand that you live in that contradiction and certainly not to claim you're perfect, but also not to be totally blind to the fact that any decision you make has an impact. It starts with awareness, and once you can be aware, then you can be on the journey toward improving that impact."

Support Certified B Corporations

B Corp Certification is becoming increasingly important for businesses that wish to acquire a reputation for concern about sustainability. According to the B Corp website, B Corp Certification for business is analogous to what Fair Trade certification is to coffee, or what USDA Organic certification is to milk. Companies wishing to acquire B Corp Certification are vetted by the nonprofit B Lab, "to meet rigorous standards of social and environmental performance, accountability, and transparency."[60]

The B Corp movement is a big one, and it is growing fast; as of this writing, over fifteen hundred companies in twenty-nine countries have become Certified B Corporations. In addition to numerous small businesses and start-ups, the list of certified B Corps includes such easily recognizable household names as Ben & Jerry's, Etsy, and Patagonia, along with less recognizable names such as Canada's Brix Media Co., Israel's Neema, London-based EQ Investors, and hundreds more.[61] (Among the companies whose CEOs contributed to this book, the list of B Corps includes Natura and Sustainable Harvest®.)

Final Word

I'll let Natura co-chairman Guilherme Leal have the last word on the subject of taking action.

"Most everything that Natura has built so far stems from a moment in the early '90s when we were going through a restructuring process. The other two founders and I sat down then to discuss what we really believed, what were our personal values, and how could we translate them into what we wanted for the business. We had this passionate belief that companies are living organisms, which could and should work to create social and environmental value. All things in our planet are interdependent, and if we want to increase our own happiness, we need to invest in growing the community's happiness and also take care of the whole of Mother Earth. So we set out to work and started figuring out, with no previous guide, how to do everything in business based on these values: how to develop products on these values, how to treat employees on these values, how to deal with suppliers and communicate with society on these values.

---

60   B Corp website: https://www.bcorporation.net/what-are-b-corps
61   B Corp website: https://www.bcorporation.net/community/find-a-b-corp

"Our ecological, social, and economic issues are a call for innovation and entrepreneurship, an opportunity to create business solutions. I believe companies that realize this, adopt triple-bottom-line management, and use business forces to promote positive impacts will have more chances to thrive. How can they start doing so? They should aim at areas that have already been tested, seek to implement the best practices, and take advantage of technologies and management tools that are already available. For example, in 2014 Natura became a B Corp, which is a very smart certification that offers companies a road map for integrating social, environmental and economic results. There's already plenty of knowledge and achievements, and much has been done, but we need to share these experiences and scale them up."

In keeping with the proverb that serves as the epigraph for this chapter, the best time for the business world to start investing in global sustainability would have been at least twenty years ago . . . but the next best time is today. The day after tomorrow will be too late—not only for the poor, not only for the ozone layer or the polar bears or the exploited South American cocoa farmers, but for business: *our* businesses, which bring incalculable value to the world and provide our livelihoods.

Don't wait. Take action today to further global sustainability . . . or look into your children's eyes tomorrow and explain why you didn't.

INDEX

APPENDIX

INTERVIEWEE PHOTOS

Andrew Liveris, Chairman and CEO
The Dow Chemical Company

Ann Sherry, CEO
Carnival Australia

Blake Mycoskie, Founder
TOMS Shoes

Cyrus Mistry, Chairman
Tata Group

Dave MacLennan, CEO
Cargill

David Griswold, CEO
Sustainable Harvest Coffee Importers

Feike Sijbesma, CEO
DSM

Francois-Henri Pinault, Chairman and
CEO Kering

Frank Dulcich, President and CEO
Pacific Seafood Company

Guilherme Leal, Co-Chairman
Natura

Jon Provisor, CIO
Guidance Production

Marc Benioff, CEO
Salesforce.com

Mike Kaplan, President and CEO
Aspen Ski Company

Mike Sangiacomo, CEO
Recology

Paul Polman, CEO
Unilever

Phil Clothier, CEO
Barrett Values Centre

Richard Branson, Founder
Virgin Group

Ryan Devlin, Co-Founder
This Bar Saves Lives

Seth Goldman, CEO
Honest Tea

Tom Szaky, Founder and CEO
TerraCycle

Walter Robb, Co-CEO
Whole Foods Market

ABOUT THE AUTHOR
MARK LEFKO

My passion for global sustainability has integrated with my professional passions by engaging business leaders in the principles and benefits of a truly sustainable organization. My name is Mark Lefko and I am the Founder and CEO of Lefko Group www.LefkoGroup.net , one of the nation's leading facilitation firms for corporate retreats, CEO peer groups, and transformative roundtables. I founded Sustainability Peer Groups www.SustainabilityPeerGroups.com , Next Step Circles www. NextStepCircles.com, and Conscious Leadership Connection www.

145

CLConnection.com which are membership organizations that engage, educate, and inspire individuals in the foundations of promoting sustainability and meaning in business and life. I have transformed my 35-year corporate background in finance and investment banking into a purpose that rises above the bottom line.

In 2014, I began writing this book on Global Sustainability to capture the global knowledge and best practices of leading companies and to prove how sustainability is shaping the growth of the most progressive and profitable Global Multinationals, Fortune 500, middle-market and start-up companies around the globe. The book was written to inspire other CEOs and executives to participate in the sustainability movement and to evolve their organizations.

Interviewing such talented and progressive CEOs and leaders equipped me with a variety of unique perspectives on global sustainability. I look forward to sharing my knowledge through speaking engagements and roundtables to enlighten individuals and management teams on the capacity of business to make the world a better place. Sharing these pioneers' insights, wisdom, and best practice experience will create an environment that helps to integrate global sustainability practices into our personal and professional lives.

For more information on booking me as a keynote speaker or to participate in one of my other programs go to www.MarkLefko.com .

A free eBook edition is available with the purchase of this book.

To claim your free eBook edition:

1. Download the Shelfie app.
2. Write your name in upper case in the box.
3. Use the Shelfie app to submit a photo.
4. Download your eBook to any device.

Shelfie

A **free** eBook edition is available
with the purchase of this print book.

CLEARLY PRINT YOUR NAME ABOVE IN UPPER CASE

Instructions to claim your free eBook edition:
1. Download the Shelfie app for Android or iOS
2. Write your name in **UPPER CASE** above
3. Use the Shelfie app to submit a photo
4. Download your eBook to any device

Print & Digital Together Forever.

Snap a photo

Free eBook

Read anywhere

CPSIA information can be obtained
at www.ICGtesting.com
Printed in the USA
BVOW08*0718200117

474037BV00002B/2/P